Falling Leaves

ADELINE YEN MAH

Level

Retold by Sue

Series Editors: Andy Hopki

Pearson Education Limited
Edinburgh Gate, Harlow,
Essex CM20 2JE, England
and Associated Companies throughout the world.

ISBN: 978-1-4058-8216-3

First published in Great Britain by Michael Joseph 1997
First published by Penguin Books Ltd 2001
This edition first published 2008

3 5 7 9 10 8 6 4 2

Typeset by Graphicraft Ltd, Hong Kong
Set in 11/14pt Bembo
Printed in China
SWTC/02

Published by Pearson Education Ltd in association with
Penguin Books Ltd, both companies being subsidiaries of Pearson Plc

For a complete list of the titles available in the Penguin Readers series please write to your local
Pearson Longman office or to: Penguin Readers Marketing Department, Pearson Education,
Edinburgh Gate, Harlow, Essex CM20 2JE, England.

Contents

Introduction

I understood that I was the least-loved child in the family because I was a girl and because my mother died giving birth to me. But I believed that if I tried hard enough, one day everyone in my family would be proud of me.

At school I came top in almost every subject. But the other pupils knew that there was something wrong. I had no toys or pretty clothes. I refused all invitations to visit anyone outside the school and never asked anyone to my house. I went to school every day carrying a terrible loneliness.

This book is a true story, about the life and family history of Adeline Yen Mah.

Adeline's childhood is a time of sadness, loneliness and fear. She is born in 1937 in the port city of Tianjin in north-east China. Her mother dies two weeks after her birth and Adeline's family members believe that she has brought them bad luck. Her father remarries one year later to a beautiful Eurasian woman who does not like his children. The family is then separated into two groups. Adeline's father, stepmother (Niang) and their two children have everything that money can buy. Adeline and her sister, Lydia, and three brothers, Gregory, Edgar and James, receive little love, attention or financial care. They become second-class citizens in their own family.

Adeline suffers terribly over the years, emotionally and physically, from her father and stepmother's treatment of her. She wants her father to be proud of her but he has no time for her. She is also bullied by Lydia and Edgar. Her brother James is her only friend.

When Adeline is still very young, she is sent away to school. She is an excellent student and wins prizes for her work. At the age of fourteen, she wins first prize in a play-writing competition for students from all over the English-speaking world. Her father finally recognizes her ability and agrees that she can study in England.

Adeline studies medicine and becomes a doctor. She returns to Hong Kong for a short time, but her relationship with her family is still difficult. With the help of a Chinese-American friend, she gets a job in a hospital in Philadelphia. She marries and has a child, but her marriage soon breaks down. Later she finds real happiness with her second husband, Bob, but the behaviour of her father and stepmother continues to shock her.

Adeline Yen Mah's story takes place during a time of great change in China and Hong Kong. At the end of the nineteenth century, foreign powers controlled large parts of China, and after the First World War the Japanese took power in much of northern China. They began to fight for more land, including Shanghai, which was heavily bombed in 1937.

After the Second World War, all foreign countries gave up their lands in China. A fight for control began between two political parties, the Chinese Communists and the Kuomintang. The Communists drove the Kuomintang out to Formosa (now Taiwan). Hong Kong, though, stayed under foreign rule, as it was rented to Britain.

Communist rule was a time of great change. By 1966, some people were criticizing the Communist leader Chairman Mao Zedong. He formed the 'Red Guard', an army of young students and workers, who stopped all complaints about the Communists. Many people were sent to work camps or killed before Chairman Mao's death in 1976.

Adeline's family moved to Hong Kong in 1948. Her father quickly built up his business again and he and Niang were important people in Hong Kong society. A small, crowded place,

Hong Kong became one of the world's great economic success stories. In 1997 the area was formally given back to the Chinese by the British, but it is still a protected area. There are controls over who can live there, even from other parts of China

Falling Leaves is a story of pain, but also of hope. Adeline fights to become independent with the support of the people who really love her, like her Aunt Baba. When Aunt Baba was dying, she asked her niece to write down the story of the family, so it would not be forgotten. Adeline found the writing painful and difficult at times. Some of the names of family members have been changed, but the story is true.

Falling Leaves has sold more than a million copies across the world. Adeline gave up medicine to write full-time. Her second book, *Chinese Cinderella*, is her life story written for children. Her third book, about the Chinese view of life, is called *Watching the Tree*.

You can find out more about Adeline Yen Mah and her work on the Internet at: www.adelineyenmah.com

Chapter 1   Changing Iron into Gold

At the Hong Kong law offices of Johnson, Stokes & Masters, we sat round an enormous shiny table and waited nervously for the reading of the will. My father's death had brought nearly the whole family together for the first time in almost forty years.

Susan, our youngest sister, was absent. She had not been invited to the funeral or to the reading of Father's will. Her name was left out of the notice that had appeared in the *South China Morning Post*. 'Joseph Tsi-rung Yen,' it read, 'dearly loved husband of Jeanne Prosperi Yen, father of Lydia, Gregory, Edgar, James and Adeline, died peacefully on 13 May 1988.'

My oldest sister, Lydia, sat close to me. My three older brothers sat together, looking serious. At the head of the table, with her lawyer, was our stepmother, who we called *Niang*, a Chinese word for mother.

At a sign from Niang, the lawyer began to speak. 'Your stepmother has asked me to inform you that your father has left no money at all.'

We looked at him in surprise. No money? This was not possible. Our father had been a very rich man, one of the most successful businessmen in Hong Kong. All our eyes turned to Niang. 'Since there is no money,' she said, 'there is no need to continue reading the will. There is nothing for any of you. Your father died penniless.'

No one said anything. Niang collected all our copies of Father's will from us and handed them back, unread, to the lawyer. We were all shocked, but not one of us questioned her. Why did we all behave like this?

To explain our unquestioning obedience that afternoon, I

have to go back to the beginning of my family's story, to its roots in nineteenth-century Shanghai.

◆

At the age of three, in 1889, my grandaunt showed her independence by refusing to have her feet bound. She pulled off the bindings each time they were put on. She finally won the argument by refusing to eat or drink until her feet were 'freed'.

At this time, Shanghai was a port city of great importance, connecting China with the rest of the world. Britain, France and the United States of America all controlled areas of the city. Great houses were built in the style of these countries. My grandfather's family lived in the French area.

My grandfather Ye Ye was the third son of the family. He was a tall, gentle Buddhist who loved poems. Grand Aunt was the youngest of the five children, the baby of the family. The older children had not been sent to school, although they did learn to read and write. But when Grand Aunt reached school age, the family was richer. She was sent to a fashionable and expensive American school, the first child in the Yen family who was taught by foreigners.

Grand Aunt never married. In those days, daughters could still be legally sold or exchanged. A wife was often used as a servant in her husband's home, especially to his mother. If she did not have a son, concubines were brought in for that purpose. Men often had sex outside the marriage, but the same behaviour by a woman could be punished by death.

I remember Grand Aunt as a tall, well-dressed woman, admired by every member of our family. Even Father and Ye Ye agreed to all her wishes.

In 1924, Grand Aunt opened her own bank, the Shanghai Women's Bank. This was very brave of her. Most men laughed at the idea of women making even simple everyday decisions. The bank was a success from the start. All the employees were women, and women of all kinds used it. Soon Grand Aunt built a large new building for the bank, in one of the best parts of the city, and her employees lived in comfortable rooms upstairs. Grand Aunt lived in a big apartment on the top floor with her friend Miss Guang. They shared a room and slept in the same bed. People talked about relationships between single women, but without serious criticism. Grand Aunt and Miss Guang employed servants and entertained expensively.

At the age of twenty-six, Grand Aunt's brother, my Ye Ye, entered into an arranged marriage. My fifteen-year-old grandmother came from a very similar Shanghai family. Across the road from Ye Ye's father's tea shop, her father owned a shop which sold many kinds of strange medicines. Ye Ye and Grandmother saw each other for the first time on their wedding day in 1903.

On the day before her wedding, Grandmother was called to see her father. 'Tomorrow you will belong to the Yen family,' she was told. 'From that moment, this is not your home. You must not contact us without permission from your husband. Your duty is to please him and his family.'

The next day the young girl, shaking with fear, was carried into her new parents' home in a red and gold chair. She wore a red dress and her face was covered with a red cloth. The wedding was noisy and colourful. Friends and relatives gave generous wedding presents.

Grandmother's fears were unnecessary, because Ye Ye was a loving and caring husband. Unusually, the young couple moved out of the Yen family home and rented their own home in the French area. I remember Grandmother as a strong-minded, intelligent woman with small feet and short hair.

When Grandmother was three years old, her feet had been bound. Her toes were forced painfully together over a number of years, stopping the foot's growth. In those days, small feet were a sign of a woman's obedience and of a family's importance. Grandmother's feet caused her pain all her life. Later, she bravely refused to cause her own daughter to suffer in this way. In 1911, when Aunt Baba was six years old, Dr Sun Yat Sen was named President of China. One of his first acts was to stop the custom of foot-binding.

My grandparents grew to love each other and had seven children. Of those, only the first two lived. Aunt Baba was born in 1905 and my father two years later. Ye Ye supported his family by hiring out boats on the busy Huangpu River. He was careful with money and by the age of forty he was quite a rich man. Then he was asked to become the manager of a business in Tianjin, a port city more than 1,500 kilometres north of Shanghai. Ye Ye had a secret. He suffered from seasickness and hated to travel in his own boats. So he decided to sell them and move to Tianjin. Not wishing to interrupt his children's schooling, Ye Ye went there alone at first.

Business in Tianjin had never been so good. British, American, European and Japanese money poured back into China after the First World War. Ye Ye was a good manager and he was well rewarded. To celebrate his good fortune, employees and friends advised him to take a young concubine to 'serve him'. Ye Ye reported this in a letter to his wife, but added that he was a 'one-woman man'.

Soon after the arrival of this letter, Grandmother and fifteen-year-old Aunt Baba hurried to join Ye Ye in Tianjin, while my thirteen-year-old father was left in the care of Grand Aunt. Aunt Baba was not allowed to continue studying, because this might harm her chances of a good marriage.

Father did well at school, especially in English. He became a Catholic during this time and was given the name Joseph. After finishing school in 1924, Father chose not to go to university.

He joined the family in Tianjin and was employed as an office boy in Ye Ye's company. Although the job was not well paid, Father learned a lot about business. Because his English was good, he was soon writing and translating important letters for the company.

Father bought an old typewriter and often typed these letters at home after dinner. His whole family stood around the dining table to watch in admiration. Ye Ye wondered about the heads of international companies who received these valuable documents. What would they think if they knew that they had been typed with one finger by an eighteen-year-old boy?

At the end of the First World War, the Japanese had been allowed to take control of some parts of China which had belonged to Germany. But they wanted more. They moved into Manchuria and into Tianjin. The Japanese army became more powerful in Tianjin, and their treatment of the Chinese was without pity. The Japanese tried to force successful Chinese businesses to work with them. They 'visited' the company that Ye Ye and Father worked for many times, and the employees were beaten. Eventually the company decided to move away.

Father did not follow the company when it moved. Instead, at the age of nineteen, he started his own business, Joseph Yen & Company, in the French part of Tianjin.

Ye Ye had such belief in his son's ability that he put all his life savings into the new company. He made Father promise to look after everyone in the family financially. Ye Ye became the new business's chief financial officer. The company did well from the start. Many businesses were moving out of Tianjin because of the Japanese, and Father bought some of them at a good price. Grand Aunt's bank also helped. The company made money from everything it did. Father began to be known in the business world as the 'magic boy' who had the power of 'changing iron into gold'.

Chapter 2   Becoming Like Each Other's Shadows

Shanghai in the 1920s was an exciting place for a young girl like Aunt Baba. Shiny motor cars sped along the roads. Enormous shops sold the latest Paris fashions, jewellery, toys, furniture and the newest things for the house. There were concerts and theatrical performances.

Aunt Baba had been sent there to work as an assistant in Grand Aunt's Women's Bank. Her close friend, Miss Ren Yong-Ping, also worked at the bank. Miss Ren was attractive, warm and full of life. She could do complicated sums in her head very quickly. When Grand Aunt checked these sums, they were always correct. Soon Miss Ren became head of her department at the bank.

On one of Father's visits to Shanghai to discuss business at the Women's Bank, he was introduced to Miss Ren. He thought that she was 'interesting'. They began to write to each other. Five months later, in 1930, they were married.

Father took his new wife to Tianjin and bought a large house in the French area. The marriage was happy, and the young couple were always together. They were 'like each other's shadows'.

Their home was large and comfortable, with running water, modern toilets and central heating. The ground floor of the house was made into offices for some of Father's employees. The rest of the family lived with Ye Ye and Grandmother upstairs. There were seven servants to look after the family, who slept at the top of the house. Father bought a large black Buick. Grandmother often went to visit her friends. On many occasions Aunt Baba took the train from Shanghai to Tianjin and stayed for long visits. There were trips to restaurants, films and shows. It was a very happy time for everyone.

Four children were born in four years. First came a daughter. The baby was large and the birth was difficult. Force had to be used and the baby's left arm was damaged. This baby was my eldest sister Jun-pei. Then came three sons: Zi-jie, Zi-lin and Zi-jun. There was a pause of three years before I (Jun-ling) came along.

At the time of my birth in 1937, the political situation in China was very difficult. In July the Japanese had attacked Tianjin and Beijing. Most of Tianjin was controlled by the Japanese. Soldiers were everywhere, causing terror among the people. Special permission was needed to cross certain parts of the city at night. So when my mother's pains began at four o'clock in the morning, Father could not take her to the Women's Hospital. Luckily, mother's great friend Dr Ting was allowed to travel freely at night, and she came to my parents' home. Dr Ting had helped at the births of all the children. My birth was quick and normal.

Dr Ting advised Father to send mother and baby to her hospital for a check and a few days' rest. Father thought this was unnecessary, as the birth had been so easy. Dr Ting then advised Father to employ a nurse to care for my mother. But Father had different ideas. He thought he and Aunt Baba could look after her, and good nurses were so expensive. A special bell was placed by mother's bedside so she could call for Father when she needed him. He did his best, but Father was not a doctor.

The headaches and fever started three days after I was born. Mother's temperature rose quickly. Her mind became confused and she could not talk clearly.

Dr Ting immediately took my mother to the Women's Hospital. Doctors tried different medicines as they fought to save her life. Her temperature rose again. She refused all food and drink. Dr Ting saw that the situation was hopeless and gave permission for her to go home to die.

Mother's condition worsened. Towards the end, her mind became clear for a short time. With Father crying by her side, she saw her children one by one, sadly calling out each of their names. To Aunt Baba she said, 'I have no more time. When I've gone, please look after our little friend here. She will never know her mother.'

My mother died two weeks after my birth. She was only thirty years old and I have no idea what she looked like. I have never seen her photograph.

◆

After my mother's death, Aunt Baba gave up her job at the Women's Bank and stayed in Tianjin to look after us. She did everything our mother had done, worrying about our meals, clothing, schooling and health. Her own chances of marriage and a family slowly disappeared.

Father, on the other hand, was now expected to marry again very soon. He was just thirty and headed his own successful company. He had worked hard and now he decided to please himself.

One afternoon he saw his secretary, Miss Wong, talking with a girlfriend. He immediately noticed that the friend was very young and very lovely.

Jeanne Virginie Prosperi was the seventeen-year-old daughter of a French father and a Chinese mother. She had beautiful white skin and large, round, dark eyes. Her hair was thick, shiny and black. She had a nice figure and was simply but beautifully dressed.

Next day at work, Father asked a few questions. He found out where Jeanne worked, drove there at lunchtime and introduced himself to her.

Jeanne's father was dead. There were five children in the family and life was not easy. Her mother did a little work at home to bring in some money. But because the children were French citizens, they were all given special help to go to French schools in the city. So although Jeanne did not come from a rich family, she had been to the best school in Tianjin. She spoke French and English. She was beautiful and she had style. Because she was half European, she was special. Father desired her.

Father drove her home from work each day. He took her to eat at expensive restaurants and to see films. They went dancing. He gave her flowers and chocolates at fast; then jewels. Jeanne asked for more and more expensive presents, and Father bought them, against Ye Ye's wishes.

Father also met Jeanne's family. Mrs Prosperi wanted the best for her beautiful daughter and was pleased with the relationship. Her eldest son had been in trouble with the police and had been sent away. Her older daughter, Reine, had just married a sensible and intelligent Frenchman. There were two other sons. Later, Father gave the older boy, Pierre, a job in his company and sent the youngest son, Jacques, to school in France.

When Father and Jeanne decided to get married, there was more expensive diamond jewellery. The wedding took place at Notre-Dame des Victoires Catholic Church. Father appeared nervous in his new jacket. Jeanne looked beautiful in her white dress and jewellery. None of us children were there. The Prosperi family brought many guests, including other children. Aunt Baba said that she, Ye Ye and Grandmother felt a little uncomfortable at the wedding party. The Chinese guests were not used to drinking alcohol. This led to embarrassment when my aunt had to leave the room more than once to be sick.

I think Jeanne was happy in the marriage at first. Ye Ye and Grandmother welcomed the idea of Father's remarriage, because it was not right for a young man to be without a wife. As I was very small, I do not know how my sister and brothers felt about it.

Father bought the house next door to ours as a present for Jeanne, and the newly married couple moved in there. The rest of the family and the servants stayed in the old house. The family ate dinner together every evening.

As my elder sister and brothers still spoke of our own dead mother as 'Mama', Grandmother told us to call Jeanne *Niang*, another word for mother. We were all given new European names by Niang. Overnight, my sister Jun-pei became Lydia, my three brothers Zi-jie, Zi-lin and Zi-jun were named Gregory, Edgar and James, and I, Jun-ling, was called Adeline.

◆

The Japanese army was now moving south. Thousands of people were killed as they took Nanking and then Shanghai. It was a time of indescribable terror which affected every family in China.

In 1939, suddenly and without warning, Tianjin was hit by a great flood. It was an enormous disaster. Two million people became homeless. Hundreds of thousands of people died either from disease or because there was nothing to eat. Schools and businesses were closed.

Because of the flood, Father built a high wooden platform connecting his two houses. Crossings were dangerous, especially for Grandmother on her small bound feet. Niang had just given birth to our half-brother, Franklin. Father had to carry her across to the 'old house' every evening, so the family could eat dinner together.

Niang had little pity for the difficulties faced by the servants. Cook had to go to market each day, and return home with food for everyone, on a roughly made wooden boat. When Ye Ye said that he thought this was very dangerous, Niang just replied that cook was a good swimmer. When the waters finally went down after forty days, Grandmother ordered the building of a covered room between the two houses. Lydia called it 'the bridge' and we used to play games there.

The youngest child of our family, our half-sister Susan, was born in November 1941. Two weeks later, across the Pacific in pearl Harbour, Japanese bombers attacked American ships. Japan was suddenly at war with America and her European friends. Japanese soldiers were ordered to take the foreign areas of Chinese cities. In one day, the fighting between Japan and China had joined with the war in Europe, spread into Malaya, brought in America, and turned the Second World War into a real world war.

Chapter 3   Disappearing Like a Spring Dream

My own memories of Tianjin are not very clear. I started at St Joseph's school in 1941. Lydia and I went there together each day.

I remember Lydia as a rather frightening figure. Six and a half years separated us in age. We were in different worlds. Lydia liked to show her power over me. She questioned me on my homework, especially religion. When I did not know the answer to a question, she hit me hard with her powerful right hand and called me stupid.

My eldest brother Gregory was a happy boy, full of life and with a good sense of fun. He was an eldest son, a favourite of Father as well as of our grandparents. Gregory was always surrounded by friends of his own age and was not very interested in me.

I feared Edgar most. He was a bully, and hit James and me. He ordered us to do things for him and took our toys and sweets.

My brother James was my only friend. We used to play together for hours and became very close. We told each other all our dreams and fears. We were both bullied by Edgar, but perhaps James suffered more because he shared a room with our two eldest brothers. When he was pushed around, he did not fight back. If he saw Edgar hitting me, he used to escape quickly and silently. When Edgar had finished and gone, James came back to me, whispering his favourite words, '*Suan le!*' ('Let it be!').

11

Niang's two children were never bullied. They were special. Franklin was Niang's favourite child. He looked very much like Niang: a handsome boy with round eyes. Susan at this time was still a baby.

I was more comfortable when I was at school with my friends. At St Joseph's, marks were added together every Friday and the girl with the highest total received a silver medal to wear for the whole week. Father immediately noticed when I wore the medal. Those were the only times when he showed that he was proud of me. At prize-giving day in 1941 I received a prize for winning the medal for more weeks than any other student in the school. It was a great moment for me, but not one of my family was there.

♦

At the beginning of 1942, the Japanese were taking an uncomfortably close interest in Father's business. They demanded that the business should be joined with a Japanese company. Father could continue to run the company, but the Japanese would take half the money that the company made. If Father refused this 'offer', he could go to prison.

After many sleepless nights, Father took a brave step. He 'disappeared'. One cold day, he took a letter to the post office and never returned home. Ye Ye continued the pretence. He went to the local police and reported that his son was missing. It was a dangerous game but it worked. Without Father, Joseph Yen & Company did not do well. No new business came in. Employees were sent home. The Japanese soon lost interest.

Father had managed to move some of his money before his disappearance, and under a false name he made his way south to Shanghai. He bought a house and soon afterwards he sent for Niang and Franklin, who travelled there with a couple of employees.

For the rest of the family, left behind in Tianjin, life was very peaceful. Aunt Baba ran the house and allowed us to invite friends home to play. Ye Ye kept a few employees in the office. On Sundays we were driven to restaurants to eat. Sometimes we were taken to see films.

After dinner one very hot day in July 1943, Grandmother had a headache. She went to her own room and lay down. Aunt Baba sat by her and told her a story. Then she left her and went to take a bath, but Ye Ye knocked urgently on the door, saying that Grandmother was ill. Doctors were called but it was too late.

I remember waking up in the great heat of a Tianjin summer morning. Aunt Baba was sitting in the bedroom, crying. She told me that Grandmother had left this world and would not come back. She had disappeared like a spring dream.

Next day there was a big funeral celebration, with music, flowers and brightly-coloured paper shapes. We children were excited by the occasion, and almost forgot its sadness.

Father was not there. He was far away in Shanghai, and very unhappy. He could not believe that his mother had died when she was just fifty-five. After that, he wore black neckties every day to remember her.

Our lives changed after Grandmother's funeral. We did not know it, but the carefree years of childhood were over.

◆

Six weeks later, Lydia, Gregory, Edgar and I left Tianjin. Father had come on the train to take us to Shanghai. Ye Ye, Aunt Baba, James and Susan stayed a little longer.

When we arrived, Father took us to the house he had bought. It had three floors, and was built in the 1920s. There was a lovely garden, with a magnolia tree covered in sweet-smelling flowers. In one corner was a wooden doghouse for Jackie, Father's guard dog.

On the ground floor were a living room and dining room, and a kitchen, bathroom and servants' rooms at the back. We children had to enter and leave the house by the back door. The first floor of the house was for Father and Niang, Franklin and Susan. We were not allowed to go into any of the rooms on the first floor. We had the second floor. Ye Ye had his own room. Aunt Baba and I shared a room, my three brothers shared another one. In the beginning, Lydia was also on 'our floor'. Later, she was given a room on the first floor, 'their floor', and went over partly to 'their side'.

♦

My new school, Sacred Heart School, was two and a half kilometres from home. On the first day, Cook took me to school on his bicycle on his way to market. Ye Ye and Aunt Baba had not yet arrived from Tianjin. In their absence, no one remembered to pick me up.

When school ended for the day, I saw anxious mothers meeting the other new children at the gate. I waited and waited, and my fear grew as I watched the other children disappear. Finally, I was the only one left. Too embarrassed to return to school, I walked out into the Shanghai streets. The crowds became thicker. I became hopelessly lost. I did not know my home address.

Shanghai in those days was not a safe place. Children were often kidnapped. Darkness fell, and I was hungry and afraid. I stood in front of a brightly lit restaurant. The owner saw me in my new school uniform and asked me to come inside. There, I saw it: the telephone! Our new Shanghai phone number had stuck in my mind. I lifted the phone. When he answered, Father was quite calm. No one had missed me.

At home again, Father said to me, 'Next time, take a map with you.'

I realized then that, without Aunt Baba, I had to look after myself. That evening, I asked Gregory to teach me how to read a map. I never got lost again.

◆

Two months later, Ye Ye, Aunt Baba, James and Susan arrived from Tianjin. I was so happy.

Niang had been separated from her daughter since Susan was only a few months old. Now, she was a beautiful two-year-old girl with big, round eyes and thick, black hair. Aunt Baba had dressed her in her best clothes to meet her mother. She looked very pretty as she ran around the sitting room, sometimes running back to Aunt Baba. Then Niang went over and tried to pick Susan up. To my little sister, her mother was a complete stranger. She fought and cried, screaming, 'I don't want you! I don't want you! Aunt Baba! Aunt Baba!'

No one dared speak. We watched silently as Susan kicked and fought in Niang's arms. Finally, Niang forced her child down on the sofa beside her and hit her hard across the face. Susan only cried louder. Out of control, Niang began to cruelly beat her daughter on her little face, ears and head. Everyone in the room was silent.

I could not understand this. I found Niang's behaviour horrible. Why did Father, Ye Ye or Aunt Baba not stop her? I knew I should keep silent, but I could not. Finally, I cried out in a shaky voice, 'Don't beat her! She's only a baby!'

Niang turned round and stared at me. For a moment, I thought she was going to come after me. Aunt Baba gave me a warning look to say nothing more. Even Susan was almost silent now. Niang had turned her terrible anger from her to me.

In those few moments, we children saw and understood everything: not only about Niang, but also about Father and Ye Ye and Aunt Baba. We had seen another side of Niang's character. After Grandmother's death, she was in total control.

15

A flood of words escaped from Niang's lips. She screamed at me: 'Get out now! How dare you open your mouth?' As I hurried to the door, she added coldly, 'I shall never forget or forgive you for this! Never! Never!'

That was how our family came together again in Father's house in Shanghai in October, 1943.

Chapter 4   Climbing a Tree to Look for Fish

Our lives changed greatly after our move. Father decided to teach us the value of money. We received no pocket money and had no clothes except for our school uniforms. We also had to walk to and from school daily. For the boys, this was a five-kilometre walk each way. Lydia's school was next to mine and was two and a half kilometres from our house. Trams ran almost from door to door.

After Ye Ye's arrival from Tianjin, we asked him for the tram fare and were each given a little money every evening. When I got off the tram at the street corner leading to the school, I had to pass several small food shops selling fresh fruit, French bread, cream cakes and other wonderful things. It was difficult for me to walk past these shops because I was always hungry and my pockets were always empty. In Tianjin Aunt Baba had allowed us to eat anything we liked for breakfast. Now we were allowed to have only one kind of breakfast: the right food for growing children, according to Niang. We were given a soup made of rice and water, with vegetables.

Others in the family had little money too. On his return to Shanghai, Ye Ye had moved all of his money from Tianjin to Father's Shanghai bank account. All the money was now in Father's name. Niang was the only other person who was able to sign for it. Like King Lear, Ye Ye signed away his fortune. Ye Ye and Aunt Baba were now penniless and had to ask Father and Niang if they wanted to buy the smallest thing.

At first, Ye Ye had a small amount of cash which he had brought with him from Tianjin. He often gave us a coin or two just to see the happiness in our eyes. He gave us our daily tram fares until his money was gone.

About two months after school started, the subject of tram fares was discussed at dinner one evening. Ye Ye spoke to Father, 'The children need a little pocket money.'

'Pocket money?' Father said, turning to Gregory and Lydia. 'Why do you need pocket money?'

'Well,' Lydia answered, 'there's the tram fare to and from school.'

'Tram fare?' Niang asked. 'Who gave you permission to ride the tram?'

'It's so far to school,' Gregory said. 'If we had to walk, it would take all day.'

'What rubbish!' Father said. 'Walking is good for you.'

Gregory complained, 'Walking is a waste of time.'

'Are you disobeying your father?' shouted Niang. 'If he decides you should walk to school, then you walk to school. Do you hear?'

There was a long silence. Then Lydia said, 'Ye Ye has been giving us our tram fares. We're used to going to school that way.'

'How dare you trouble Ye Ye for money?' Niang demanded. 'You must not go to anyone else for money. All of you! If you think you need money, come to me. Money doesn't grow on trees. We're going to teach you a lesson . . .' She paused. 'If you want your tram fares, you must each come to us and apologize. If you ask for your tram fare very nicely, we might give it to you. You'll get it only if you show that you are very sorry.'

So we all started walking to school and back every day. We understood that the question of tram money and the question of power in the family went together. We wanted to show that, to us, Ye Ye was still the head of the family, not Niang.

Lydia was the first to change her mind. Within two weeks, I noticed that she was arriving home from school earlier. I knew that she had given in to Niang. When winter came, the walk to school became too difficult for my brothers. One by one, they made their apologies and received their tram fares.

Through all my years in Shanghai, I could never make myself go to Niang and ask for the tram fare. I continued to walk to school and had to listen to the cruel things the other schoolchildren said as they got into waiting cars at the end of the day. They whispered that I took my own private 'number eleven tram' daily to school, meaning that my legs carried me.

Father had strict rules for other parts of our lives, too. Lydia and I were not allowed to have long hair, only sensible, old-fashioned haircuts. For the three boys it was much worse. They were forced to have their heads shaved completely. This was Father's idea, to show us that life was not all fun. The whole school laughed at them.

Life was very different for Franklin and Susan. A private teacher, Miss Chien, looked after them. They had lots of lovely new clothes and toys. Franklin's hair was fashionably cut. They ate their meals separately in their room, and ordered whatever they liked from the kitchen. Every afternoon they had tea with sandwiches and cakes.

Miss Chien acted as a spy, reporting back our conversations and activities to Father and Niang. She became friends with Lydia. Lydia was the only one of us who ever had afternoon tea with them.

◆

At the age of sixty-five, Ye Ye found himself without a penny. Father made it clear that Ye Ye and Baba must ask Niang for any money they wanted. This was an insult to Ye Ye. Gently Ye Ye refused, telling Baba he was not going to 'climb a tree to look for fish'.

Instead, father and daughter visited Grand Aunt at the 'Women's Bank and Aunt Baba asked for her old job back. Baba did not tell Grand Aunt the real reason why she wanted her job back. To protect his son from public criticism, Ye Ye made her promise never to tell anyone.

Father and son never discussed money again. Aunt Baba returned to work. On pay days, she took her pay in cash and placed half the bank notes in Ye Ye's writing desk. This was the only money that Ye Ye had.

Aunt Baba was like a mother to me. Now we were even closer, and she looked after me in every way. Most of all, she cared about my progress at school, checking my homework every evening and helping me with tests. She wanted me to go to college – the ticket to escape and independence. I understood that I was the least-loved child in the family because I was a girl and because my mother died giving birth to me. But I believed that if I tried hard enough, one day everyone in my family would be proud of me.

At school, I came top in almost every subject. But the other pupils knew that there was something wrong. I never spoke about my family. I had no toys or pretty clothes. I refused all invitations to visit anyone outside the school and never asked anyone to my house. I went to school every day carrying a terrible loneliness.

♦

One day we had a pleasant surprise when one of Father's work colleagues came to visit and brought a gift. It was a large box with seven little ducklings inside. As usual, Franklin and Susan chose theirs first. I was last. I was left with the weakest little bird, which had a very small head but was soft and yellow. I fell in love with it immediately.

I was about eight years old. My duckling was everything to me. I ran home from school each day to take her in my hands and carry her lovingly into our bedroom. I did my homework while the duckling walked around our beds.

One day I was in the garden looking for insects for the duckling's dinner. I came too close to Jackie, Father's guard dog. He rushed over noisily and showed his sharp teeth. I tried to calm him by putting out my hand to him, but he sank his teeth into my left wrist. I got away and ran to my room. Aunt Baba looked after my cut wrist and calmed me. Jackie was *their* favourite pet. It would be best to say nothing, cause no trouble.

That evening it was warm and Father decided that we should all go and sit out in the garden. Jackie had been receiving obedience training and Father wanted to test the dog.

'Let's test Jackie on one of those ducklings that were given to the children,' said Father. I felt a horrible fear as he turned to my oldest brother: 'Go and fetch one of the ducklings.' Immediately I knew that the chosen duckling would be mine.

Gregory did not look at me as he came back and handed my duckling to Father. A wave of sickness swept over me. The duckling looked so small. Jackie greeted my Father happily. Father sat on a chair. Everyone else was there, watching. I shook as Father put the duckling carefully down on the grass and I felt my heart breaking.

Jackie was ordered to 'sit' about two metres away. He sat quietly for a few moments. Then the duckling saw me. She made a little noise and moved towards me. In one powerful jump, Jackie had the duckling's left leg between his teeth. Father rushed over, angry at Jackie's disobedience. Immediately, Jackie let the duckling go, but the damage was done.

I ran over and picked up my pet. Her leg was hanging loosely from her body. A greater loneliness than I had ever known swept over me. I carried her to my room, placed her gently on my bed and lay down next to her. I spent that night with her in an unhappiness so great that I could not talk about it even to my aunt.

The duckling refused to eat or drink and died early the next morning. James and I put her in a hole under the magnolia tree in the garden. The tree was covered with flowers. Even today, every time I smell the sweet smell of magnolias I experience again a terrible feeling of sadness.

Chapter 5   Obeying and Disobeying

When I was ten years old, two events happened within a few days that worsened my relationship with Niang.

One of my schoolfriends invited me to go to her birthday party. It was on a celebration day for Catholics: a special holiday for our school but not for the other schools. I knew I was not allowed to visit my friends in their homes, but I thought I could go secretly if I planned it very carefully.

On the morning of the party, I dressed in my school uniform and carried my book bag with me as normal. I spent a wonderful morning at my friend's house, playing with her toys. Then midday arrived and I was expected to go home for lunch. I told my friends I would be back in an hour. They asked me for my home phone number, and I gave it without thinking.

I went home happily and ran into my bedroom. There, unexpectedly, I came face to face with Niang.

She was surprised. 'Why are you home so early?'

'Well, lessons finished a little early,' I lied.

She did not believe me. 'Come here!' she commanded. She searched me and found some money that Aunt Baba had given me. I was going to use it to buy a birthday present for my friend.

'Where did this come from?' she asked.

I could not say Aunt Baba's name. I told some lies. Niang hit me and asked more questions. She thought I had stolen the money. She hit me again.

Then the telephone rang. The servant appeared at the door.

'Sorry to interrupt you, Mrs Yen,' she said. 'There is a telephone call for her . . .' She pointed at me.

I suddenly remembered that my friends were waiting for me to continue our game. Niang hurried to the phone and I could hear her voice.

'Adeline's busy right now. This is her mother. Who is calling, please? . . . You are waiting for her? But don't you have to be at school today? A holiday! How nice! . . . I'm afraid Adeline won't be able to return to your house this afternoon. Don't wait for her.'

She came back and looked angrily at me. 'You are a thief and a liar. You have bad blood from your mother. I don't think you deserve to live here. You belong in an orphanage!'

As my world crashed around me, she told me to stay in my room until my father got home. 'And you'll have nothing to eat until this matter is decided.'

Later, Father came into my room in a serious mood, carrying a dog whip. I could not lie to him, and I told him that Aunt Baba had given me the money. He ordered me to lie face down on my bed and he whipped my bottom and my legs. As I lay shaking with pain and fear, I saw a rat run across the floor. I wanted to scream, but kept silent.

Father then hung the whip over his arm and said that Aunt Baba and I would have to be separated.

◆

Two days later, the second terrible event happened. I had been top of my class for four years, and now I was voted class president.

I walked home from school happy, forgetting my troubles for a few moments. A large group of my schoolfriends had decided secretly to follow me home and give me a surprise celebration party.

Five minutes after I entered the house, the doorbell rang. The servant answered the door to a group of laughing girls, all asking to see me. The servant took the girls into the living room and climbed the stairs to my room.

There was a frightened look on her face as she whispered to me, 'A crowd of your friends has come from school to see you. They've asked for you.'

'Is Niang home?' I asked.

'I'm afraid so. And your father too.'

As I went quietly down the stairs to greet my friends, I could hear twelve ten-year-old girls laughing loudly through the whole house.

My schoolfriends were too happy and excited to notice my white-faced silence. They surrounded me, shouting out their congratulations. My stomach turned over. 'I'm only ten years old,' I thought. 'Surely Niang can't kill me for this.'

The servant reappeared in the doorway. 'Your mother wants to see you *now.*'

I excused myself and went upstairs. I knew this was going to be terrible. As I stood in front of my parents, we could hear the girls laughing from downstairs.

'Who are those people, and who invited them here?' Niang demanded loudly.

'They are my friends. No one invited them. They came to celebrate with me because I've become class president.'

'Is this party your idea?'

'No, Niang. I had no idea.'

'Come here!' she screamed. She hit my face so hard that I was knocked over. 'You're lying! You planned it, to show off our house to your penniless schoolfriends.'

23

I began to cry. Niang continued to scream at me, and hit me again. 'Go downstairs now and tell them to leave the house. They are not welcome here.'

I left the room and went downstairs. There was now silence among my friends. They had heard every word. I stood in front of them, unloved and unwanted by my own parents, my face covered in tears and blood. I tried to speak as calmly as possible. 'I'm sorry. My father wishes to sleep. They ask me to tell you to go home.'

One special friend, Wu Chun-mei, took out her handkerchief and handed it to me. I saw the loving sadness in her eyes. With tears pouring down my face, I said, 'Thank you all for coming. I shall never forget your kindness.' They left the room, leaving the presents they had brought me.

As Wu Chun-mei passed the stairs, she shouted up, 'You are unfair and cruel! I'll tell my father!'

Father made me throw all the presents away. He and Niang said that I had asked all my friends to come to the house to insult them. He was very angry.

'What's going to happen to me?' I asked fearfully.

'We're not sure,' was Father's cruel reply. 'Since you're not happy here, you must go somewhere else.' I dropped to my knees in front of them and apologized. I knew that I had no choice. They had the money and the power.

◆

My elder sister Lydia did not do well in school. With her damaged left arm, her future did not look hopeful. Father and Niang decided to arrange a marriage for her.

On their next visit to Tianjin they took Lydia and introduced her to Samuel Sung, the younger son of our family doctor in Tianjin. He had been studying in America, but had now returned and was looking for a wife. He was already thirty-one years old, not good-looking, but intelligent.

Many years later, Lydia wrote down her side of the story:

When I was seventeen, Father called me to their bedroom to talk to me. They told me to stand in front of the mirror and look at myself. I did not understand (because I did not find anything unusual about my appearance), but they told me to look closely at my left hand, which was a strange shape.

Father said, 'We have found a man for you to marry. It is a good chance, because if you do not marry now, you will not be able to find anyone who wants you later.'

I looked at myself and saw that I was truly not very good-looking with my damaged left hand. I had never even thought of marriage at seventeen. I admired my schoolfriends who were going for further studies abroad. But I heard Niang's cold voice: 'I'm not going to keep another old unmarried woman in my house! You must do as we say!' I was a fool. I thought I had to obey them.

Lydia and Samuel had a big wedding in 1948, with over five hundred guests. Months before the wedding, presents started to arrive. The best ones were kept by Niang.

Lydia moved with Samuel to Tianjin after the wedding and lived with Samuel's parents. I did not see them again for thirty-one years.

◆

My brothers Gregory and Edgar had found their own ways to solve the problem of having no money.

Playing in their room one day, I found a box under Gregory's bed. It contained some notepaper and envelopes from the school and some ink. James told me that Gregory had made friends with an employee in the school financial office, and was printing letters on official school paper asking for small amounts of money. Gregory's friend gave him cash for these payments. This gave him a regular stream of pocket money.

At the same time, Ye Ye had started to notice that banknotes were disappearing from his desk drawer. But he kept silent about this, as he did not want to make trouble for any of us.

One day things went wrong for Edgar, who was the thief. He had taken a few American dollars from Ye Ye's desk and changed them for local money. This was the time when Chinese notes had very little value. Edgar was given an enormous bag full of Chinese banknotes. He had so much money that he did not know where to hide it.

He dug a large hole in the garden, put all the money into it, and covered it over again. He thought his secret was safe, but he had forgotten Father's dog, Jackie.

Next day, while we were at school, Jackie started digging in the place where the money was hidden. Soon banknotes were flying about all over the garden.

Niang told the servants to pick up the money and tidy the garden. Not a word was said until the end of dinner. Then, instead of the usual fruit bowl, the servants brought in a large plate piled with Chinese money.

Father took Edgar upstairs and hit him repeatedly with Jackie's whip. We sat in Ye Ye's room, listening to the awful sounds of the beating and Edgar's cries of pain.

♦

Ye Ye and Father were happy when the Japanese lost the war in 1945 and left China. They soon had new worries, though. Almost immediately, a war began within the country, between the Kuomintang* and the Communists.† Newspapers were full

---

* The Kuomintang: the Nationalist People's party in China. It formed the government in southern China after the First World War.

† The Communist party: a political party which began in China in the 1920s. It grew in power and became the enemy of the Kuomintang. The Communist soldiers became known as the Red Army.

of stories of the terrible acts that were being carried out by the Communists against business people and people with property. By 1948 the economic situation for people like my father was looking very bad. Businessmen were sending all their money to Hong Kong, the United States and Europe.

On the day following my schoolfriends' disastrous visit, Father suddenly made a rare appearance on the second floor (our floor) and visited Aunt Baba and Ye Ye. He told them that he and Niang had decided to move to Hong Kong with Franklin and Susan. Would Ye Ye and Baba go too? Ye Ye accepted his son's invitation.

Aunt Baba decided to stay in Shanghai. She did not want to give up her job and live with Niang's daily criticism. Communism could not be worse than a life under Niang. She asked what would happen to us. Father said he would leave his three teenage sons in their Shanghai schools, and then send them to university in England.

'That leaves Adeline,' Ye Ye said. 'What will you do with her?'

'She has become very difficult,' Father said. 'She must be taught a lesson. We have decided to take her away from you and send her to school in Tianjin. She will not be allowed to send or receive letters. She must learn obedience!' Father rushed from the room.

'What's all this about?' Aunt Baba asked Ye Ye. 'The child has done nothing. It will break her heart to be taken away from us.'

Ye Ye explained. 'The child has done no wrong. But every day she annoys them just by being there. They're sending her away because they want to be rid of her.'

Chapter 6   Offering the Same Treatment to All?

Father and Niang took me north to Tianjin in September 1948. One part of the country after another was being lost to the Red

Army in the war, and most people were running away in the opposite direction.

Tianjin was full of people who had been made homeless by the fighting. They brought disease with them. The city could not take all these people, and soon they were forced to live in rough camps outside the city.

There were only about one hundred pupils left at St Joseph's School when Niang took me there. Only four of us lived in the school; the rest were day girls. Over the next few weeks, the number of girls fell. Soon we were all in one classroom, all ages from seven to eighteen. No Chinese was spoken during school hours. We all had to speak in English or French.

I was unhappy. Chinese had been the language of my school in Shanghai. I was lonely and wanted only to return to Aunt Baba. I poured out my feelings in long letters, asking for a few kind words from home. No letter ever came. I did not know of my parents' rule that I must receive no visitors, no phone calls and no letters.

Without any contact with the outside world, I did not know that the Communists had taken Manchuria and were now moving towards Beijing and Tianjin. Many students and their families escaped to Taiwan and Hong Kong. There were no more classes. We spent our time reading English books of our choice.

More and more girls left the school as the Communist armies came nearer. Eventually, I was the only student left there. I spent every Sunday and every holiday alone in the school, including Christmas and New Year. The nuns did not know what to do with me. I remember that Christmas, sitting in the enormous dining room, eating Christmas dinner by myself.

On 31 January 1949, the Communists marched into Beijing without firing a shot. Tianjin was taken at about the same time.

My sister Lydia was living in Tianjin with her husband Samuel and his parents during the time I was at school there. They never visited me or asked about me. When they escaped to Taiwan, they left me behind without making contact.

Day after day I sat alone in the library wondering what was going to happen to me. There were no more classes. I was the only child there.

Suddenly one morning, Niang's sister Aunt Reine appeared in the entrance to my school. She was my first visitor. I began to cry when I saw her. She was preparing to leave Tianjin with her husband and two children when she remembered that I was still at St Joseph's. She decided, without asking anyone, to take me out of school.

Outside, the streets were very quiet. I saw Communist soldiers dressed in thick winter uniforms. We walked the short distance to Father's two houses on the Shandong Road. At that time, all Niang's relatives were living in Father's Tianjin houses. It was strange to be back in my old home. I met Uncle Jean Schilling and their two children, Victor and Claudine. They invited me to play with them. Aunt Reine noticed my nervousness. She placed her arm around me and whispered, 'Don't worry, I will offer the same treatment to all three of you.'

Over dinner, Uncle Jean explained that my parents were in Hong Kong and we were going to join them there as soon as possible. A few days later, the Schilling family and I boarded a ship for Hong Kong.

◆

Back in Shanghai, my aunt enjoyed a time of peace and happiness. The Communist soldiers were polite and helpful. They kept law and order. Shops and businesses reopened. Public services were better managed than before.

Aunt Baba looked after my three brothers, who were still at school in Shanghai. The days were calm and well-organized. Aunt Baba watched the boys leave for school in the morning before going to work herself. The boys were now given a fair amount of pocket money.

There were two servants and Miss Chien. Miss Chien was an unmarried woman in her thirties. When Franklin and Susan went to Hong Kong, she feared she would be sent away. So she prepared tasty meals for Aunt Baba and made clothes for them all.

Gregory and Edgar finished school in Shanghai and went to England for further studies. James stayed at school for another year and Aunt Baba looked after him lovingly. He was good company for my aunt. They often read Ye Ye's letters together. In Shanghai James was free to do as he liked, and when Father sent for him to go to Hong Kong he did not want to go. When he finally left, travelling was difficult. James and Uncle Frederick (our own dead mother's younger brother) travelled to Canton. They did not have the papers that were needed to cross into Hong Kong. They went secretly across in an old boat at night. They were lucky, and made the journey safely.

Back in Shanghai, Aunt Baba was now left alone with two servants and Miss Chien.

◆

Father, Niang, Ye Ye, Franklin and Susan were living in a second-floor flat on Boundary Street in Kowloon. In 1949, Hong Kong was a sleepy, tidy, quiet little city with clean streets and little traffic.

Aunt Reine had succeeded in bringing Niang's diamonds out of Tianjin in secret. She had covered the stones with cloth and used them as buttons on her winter coat. As she cut them free, the jewels fell one by one on to the coffee table. Niang was so happy about this that she did not seem too angry about my unexpected appearance.

Day after day Niang took the Schilling family sightseeing in the large family car. I was left behind with Ye Ye and the servants. Secretly I was pleased. It was wonderful to be with Ye Ye again.

We went for walks and played games. I read the newspapers to him every morning. Often we just sat quietly together, happy with each other's company.

At Sunday breakfast, Niang suggested that we should all have lunch at an expensive hotel on Hong Kong Island. Everyone squeezed into Father's large car. I was the only one left at home, standing by the side of the road with the servants.

Victor complained. 'It's not fair, Mother,' he said to Aunt Reine. 'Why is Adeline never allowed to go anywhere with us?'

Niang interrupted. 'The car is too crowded. There is no room for Adeline. She is staying here. You can come with us now or you can stay at home with her.'

'Then I think I'll keep Adeline company.' Victor climbed out of the car and stood by my side as the car drove away. I have never forgotten his thoughtfulness.

Uncle Jean and his family soon left for Geneva, where he had a new job.

◆

It did not take Father long to make a name for himself in the business life of Hong Kong. He quickly started some very successful companies.

Father and Niang were soon important people in the high society of Hong Kong. Unusually for Chinese people, they spoke English and were comfortable with Westerners. Niang was beautiful and fashionable, and she appeared often in the society pages of local newspapers and magazines. Wonderful dinners were held at home. During these dinners, Ye Ye and we stepchildren were never talked about or introduced to any of the important visitors. We had to stay hidden in our rooms, and not embarrass anyone by our presence.

Two days after the Schilling family departed, Niang ordered me to pack my things. I was being taken away.

Chapter 7   Dreaming of Magic Lands

The Sacred Heart School and Orphanage, run by Italian nuns, was on Hong Kong Island, facing the sea. We climbed up the stone steps to the entrance and were greeted by Mother Mary and Mother Louisa.

Sacred Heart was one of the few schools which took boarders and orphans. The two groups were dressed in different uniforms and were not allowed to mix with each other. The orphans did not attend classes but were taught to do cooking and cleaning and to wash clothes. My future was in Niang's hands. I did not know if she would leave me at the school as an orphan or as a boarder.

She and Franklin went into a private room with the two nuns and talked for a long time. The waiting was horrible. Finally, they came out. I was surprised when Niang smiled and touched me kindly on the head. This was the only time she ever touched me when I was a child. 'How lucky you are!' she said. 'Mother Mary has agreed to allow you to join the boarding school in the middle of the school year!'

There were sixty-six boarders at the school. Each child was given a number. We each had our own space in an enormous cupboard in the dining room. Each boarder kept the food sent from home in her space. Everyone could see the amount of food a girl received. It was a measure of the love your family had for you. During my years at the school, my space was always empty.

Eggs were special. They were brought from home and kept in the kitchen. Each boarder painted her number on the outside of the egg. For breakfast we all had bread, butter and jam. Mother Mary then brought in a big container full of hot, freshly boiled eggs. She picked up the eggs one by one and placed them in egg cups, reading out the numbers. You walked up to her when you heard your number and collected your egg.

If your number was called by Mother Mary, it meant that someone from home loved you enough to bring you eggs for your breakfast. The breakfast egg, more than anything, separated us into two groups: the loved ones and the unloved ones. I, of course, was eggless during the whole of my stay at Sacred Heart.

We had lessons from eight in the morning to midday, and from one-thirty to three-thirty. Tea was served in the dining room at four. This was the hour when the difference between the haves and the have-nots really showed. As well as the usual bread, butter and jam, out came the chocolates, cakes and fruit that had been brought in during Sunday visiting hours.

On birthdays, the birthday girl was allowed to wear a pretty dress instead of school uniform. She stood next to Mother Mary behind an enormous birthday cake. We sang 'Happy Birthday'. The cake was cut up and the birthday girl went around the room, giving out her cake. She then opened her presents in front of everyone.

I always went into tea a little late, ate my bread, butter and jam as fast as possible, and ran out of the room. I knew there would never be a birthday celebration for me. I would never be able to give anyone a piece of my cake. My friend Mary Suen and I did not speak to each other about this, but I often found some good things from her laid out on my plate: a few sweets or a piece of fruit.

Mary was not very clever at her lessons, and often had to ask me for help, but in other ways she was as wise as someone much older. She was especially kind to me because she herself came from an unhappy family.

After tea there was an hour of free time. I usually visited the library. This was magic for me. There were books on every subject under the sun. When the library closed, I came out with my arms full of books.

Once I helped Mary solve a mathematical problem, and my

answer proved to be more correct than the one in her schoolbook. The story spread and soon other boarders came to me when they had problems with their homework. They started not to notice that my only Sunday dress was too small for me, that my space in the food cupboard stayed empty and that I was never given an egg.

Sundays were visiting days. In the beginning I was as excited as everyone else while I prepared for my family. Of course I had no visitors. The other boarders gave me pitying looks. It was clear that I was the only truly unwanted daughter.

After a time, on Sundays mornings I picked up a pile of books and quietly went into the toilet. I stayed there reading until I heard my friends returning, carrying presents and food, trying on new clothes and shoes. Then I quietly came out and joined them.

It was a sad time for me and I often lay awake at night, full of worries about my future. Sometimes I heard the sound of a great ship leaving for the sea. I saw myself standing on one of these ships, journeying through dark waters to a magical land: England or America.

♦

In the summer of 1951, I became ill. I started coughing up blood, had a fever and had difficulty breathing. After two days I was taken to hospital. At first the doctors thought I was going to die. They informed my family.

I was lonely and afraid. No one came from home. Mary was my only visitor. I was deeply grateful for her visits and the gifts of food she brought me. Slowly my fever lessened.

One day, at lunchtime, Father suddenly appeared. Mary had gone home to eat. He stood by my bed looking at me.

'How are you feeling?' he asked.

'I'm much better, Father,' I told him. Pleasure, fear and surprise meant that I could think of nothing else to say. Father had the same difficulty. He watched me for a few minutes in silence, touched me on the head, said, 'Take care,' and left.

A nurse and Mary walked in at that moment. 'Who was *that?*' the nurse asked.

I answered proudly, 'That's my father.'

She was surprised. 'We thought you were an orphan.'

'Almost an orphan, but not quite.'

'Me too,' Mary told the nurse. 'I'm the same.'

At that moment I felt very close to my schoolfriend.

◆

Ye Ye was lonely in Hong Kong. He spoke no English or Cantonese and had no friends. He had difficulties communicating with the servants. Franklin was rude to him and Susan was too young to interest him. If he wanted to buy any small thing, he had to ask for money from Father. He looked old and sad.

When Ye Ye became ill, Father ordered him to eat special meals. He was now only allowed to eat boiled fish, plain rice and a few vegetables. This same meal was given to him three times a day, and he hated it. He demanded to move out and live on his own. This was refused. He wrote to Aunt Baba that he wanted to return to Shanghai and spend his last years with her. This was also impossible.

Ye Ye's letters to Aunt Baba became sadder. 'We all want to live,' he wrote, 'but some things are worse than dying: being lonely or bored, suffering pain. I have worked hard all my life. Now I wonder what it was all about. In this house, where I count for nothing, each day passes like a year. Could death really be worse?'

Ye Ye died on 27 March 1952. Father was too busy to inform Aunt Baba himself. Instead, she received the news from a letter written by one of Father's employees.

Chapter 8 Planning a Brighter Future

At Ye Ye's funeral, I started to cry when I saw his photograph and I could not stop the tears. No one else was crying. My tears were annoying Niang.

'What are *you* crying about?' she suddenly whispered angrily. Then she turned to Father. 'I do think Adeline is getting uglier as she grows older. Just look at her!'

We returned to the house after the funeral, and Niang called me into the living room. She wore an expensive black suit. She stared at my old school uniform. I felt small and plain.

'Sit down, Adeline,' she said in English. I waited to hear what she had to say.

'Your father has seven children to support,' she began. 'We must think of your future. What plans do you have?'

I said something about hoping to attend university in England, like my brothers.

'Your father,' she interrupted, 'does not have endless amounts of money. We have decided you should study to be a secretary and find yourself a job.'

Thinking of my report card with all its 'A's, I knew that Niang would try to make sure that I never had a future.

Back at school, I wrote letter after letter to Niang and Father, asking them to allow me to go to London with James. I had made up my mind to go to college. There was no reply.

Then one Saturday afternoon about a month later, Mother Valentino came to me with the news that the family car was outside waiting for me. I asked myself what I had done wrong now.

But my luck had changed. Seven months earlier, I had entered a play-writing competition. The competition was open to students from all over the English-speaking world. I did not know it, but I had won first prize. The story reached the newspapers. Father was going up in the lift to his office that morning when an employee showed him the newspaper. 'Is the winner, Adeline Jun-ling Yen, a relative?' he asked. 'You have the same uncommon last name.' Proudly, Father read and reread the story. That afternoon he sent for me.

Arriving home, I went to see Father. He showed me the newspaper. I could not believe it! I had won! Father wanted to talk to me about my future.

'I know you want to go to university,' he said. 'It seems you have some ability. What subjects do you wish to study?'

'I think I'd like to study literature,' I said bravely. 'I'll become a writer.'

'A writer!' he laughed. 'What sort of writer? No, I've thought about it and made a decision. You will go to England with James to study medicine.'

I quickly agreed. I would do anything he advised if I could go to England.

That night James and I talked until late. We were full of plans, hopes and fears. Father and Niang had been out to a dinner party. When Niang got back and found us, she did not look pleased. 'What are you two doing wasting electricity and laughing at this time of night?' she demanded. 'You waste your father's money all the time.' She switched off the light and left the room, shutting the door loudly behind her.

'Whatever problems we have in England,' James said, 'they can't possibly be worse than this!'

◆

In January 1949, Lydia escaped from Tianjin to Taiwan with her husband Samuel and his parents. Samuel's father, our family doctor in Tianjin, soon started work in Taipei. He began a relationship with a younger woman and openly made her his concubine. The situation became very difficult for Samuel's mother. After a bitter argument, she left and returned to Tianjin.

At that time, most work in Taiwan was in farming and fishing. There were few jobs, and Samuel could not find suitable employment. After the birth of a daughter, they decided to follow Samuel's mother and return to Tianjin.

Father tried to advise them not to go back to China. Repeatedly he warned them of the hard life they would have under the Communists.

A few months after their return, Samuel was taken away to prison. His father had been a well-known political figure in the Kuomintang. Samuel therefore had to be questioned. While he was in prison, Lydia and their daughter lived with Samuel's mother. The two women did not like each other and were not happy living together.

When Samuel was freed after six months, they decided to move into one of Father's two houses on Shandong Road, with Niang's Aunt Lao Lao.

When Niang found out that they were living there, she was very angry and told Father to make them move out. When he tried to do this, Samuel and Lydia attacked back. They warned Father that they had found out that Father's employees were guilty of certain illegal money exchanges. If Father made them move out, they would tell what they knew. They demanded and received some money. They stayed in Father's house but he never forgave them.

With the difficulties of living under Communism and the argument with her family, Lydia became more and more angry. She blamed her problems on her husband and began to hate him. They continued to share the same bed, but had different dreams.

◆

In August 1952, James and I sailed to England. I found it difficult to believe my good luck. We were at last on a wonderful journey of discovery and independence. I remembered the long nights at boarding school when I had dreamed of a journey like this.

James repeated a well-known Chinese saying: 'Mountains are high and rivers are long. Is anything impossible?'

We made friends with the small group of Chinese students on the ship. Life was full of hope for us.

Chapter 9　Doing the Impossible

After James and I left for England, Franklin became more and more important in the house. Niang gave him everything he wanted. He had large amounts of pocket money, while Susan was not given a penny.

One day, when he was thirteen, Franklin was being driven home from a birthday party. They drove past a field of strawberries and Franklin saw boxes of the freshly picked fruit. He stopped the car and bought two large boxes. On the long drive home, he ate every strawberry.

A few days later, his throat hurt and he had a fever. He went out in the sun. Half an hour later he came in, complaining of a bad headache. He got into bed and asked Susan to bring him a glass of water. When Susan brought the water, he complained that it was not cold enough and threw the glass at her.

When Niang came home, Franklin was very ill and was making strange sounds. An ambulance took him to the hospital. He could not drink. The doctor spoke to my parents. Franklin had a very dangerous disease which affected the brain. He had probably caught it from eating those unwashed strawberries. Father visited him every day. Niang almost lived in his hospital room. Slowly, Franklin appeared to improve.

The most important social event of the season – a dance – was happening soon. Niang very much wanted to go. She talked to the doctor. He said her son appeared a little better and her social life should not stop because of Franklin's illness.

It was a great occasion. Niang was dancing, wearing a shiny green dress and green earrings, when she was called to the telephone. It was the doctor, who sounded tired and upset. Franklin had suddenly become worse and was dead.

Niang was never the same after Franklin's death. She did not turn to Father, or to her daughter, for emotional support. She had shown little love before, but even that died with her son.

◆

I had studied photographs of London in my school library but was unprepared for the sight of the terrible damage that had been done to the city by the Second World War.

Gregory and Edgar were also in London. They had found few science courses to study at their schools, but eventually, Gregory went to Imperial College to study mechanical engineering and Edgar to medical school.

Father had arranged for me to attend a boarding school in Oxford. It was a school for young ladies, and no science courses were offered. Instead, we learned music, dancing and riding. I left there and went to a school in London, took extra courses over the summer and passed the necessary examinations for medical school. At the age of seventeen, I started at University College in London, where my brother Edgar was already studying.

Edgar was the least physically attractive of my three brothers. He had a square face, small eyes and thin lips. Edgar was nobody's favourite. When we were children, he showed his unhappiness by bullying me, the youngest. He did not like it when my father was proud of my success. At first he was one year ahead of me at medical school. But then he failed one of his examinations and we had to take some classes together. Eventually, he began to hate me. At college, he told the other students that he did not know me.

♦

In the 1950s there was much racial prejudice in England. There were few Chinese students, and the English students were not used to being so close to a Chinese person. Some of them felt uncomfortable with me. Some were insulting or rude.

Less than one-fifth of our class of medical students were female. Most of us were serious and hard-working. The boys did not like it when we received good marks. Some said quite openly that all female medical students were ugly. Others said that we were 'robbing' males of entry into medical school.

Sometimes it was difficult not to notice the racial and sexual insults. Often, I sat and ate lunch alone while the other students sat in friendly groups on other tables. Once when I was brave enough to take my lunch to their table, a boy came and quickly took the last seat. I went to get another chair. Silence fell around me. Everyone ate as quickly as possible and left. I was alone, surrounded by dirty dishes and empty chairs.

I had problems, but it was still a wonderful time. The whole world of science was opening to me. I could not wait to get to classes every morning. I studied hard and dreamt of making my father proud of me.

Some of my friends at medical school were Jews. With them I suffered no prejudice and felt like an equal. They invited me to their homes and never said hurtful things about the Chinese. We discussed our studies and ate in Chinese restaurants.

James was now studying engineering at Cambridge University. I often visited him on Sundays, when we spent pleasant afternoons drinking coffee and talking in his rooms. I was excited and proud to walk the streets of Cambridge beside my tall and handsome brother.

◆

I had another, secret friend. He was Dr Karl Decker, one of my
university professors. I was seventeen and he was thirty-four. He
was a German who spent long hours working. He too was
intelligent, tall and handsome.

He began to say nice things about my clothes and appearance.
For months I could not believe that Dr Decker admired me.
How could a great scientist be interested in a teenage Chinese
medical student? But he spent hours discussing his work with
me, and he wrote long letters to me about his life, his memories
and his problems. He wrote about music, poems, ideas and how
much he wanted me.

We were on dangerous ground. Couples of mixed race were
rare in those days and we did not seem to belong together. Our
meetings were mostly private. Karl did not want his colleagues to
know that he was seeing one of his students, a Chinese girl. I did
not want my friends and family to know about him.

It was an impossible situation but it continued. We were very
different, but our love for each other was strong. Some evenings
when Karl's work was finished, we sat together and talked until
late at night. At these moments, we were as close as a woman and
a man can be.

Sometimes I was frightened by Karl's complicated emotions.
'It's all so sad and difficult,' he told me, adding, 'of course, you
shouldn't be spending time with me. You! You who are so full of
life and hope!'

Karl told me that that I should go out with Chinese boys of
my own age. When I did so, sometimes he even came along to
see what the boys were like. One evening, I was sitting between a
Chinese friend and Karl in a dark cinema. Karl suddenly reached
over and touched my hand gently.

◆

My Chinese friends were important to me. Among them, I could be myself. I could speak my own language and relax with people who could laugh at the same things. There were Chinese students from China and Hong Kong, and from Singapore, Malaysia, Indonesia and Mauritius.

An important person in our lives was C. S. Tang, the president of the Chinese students' organization. He was very handsome and was studying at Imperial College. Politically, he supported the left. Unlike the rest of us, he intended to return home to China to live and work. He rented Chinese films showing the wonderful work done by the Communist fighters. One day, C. S. told me, 'In everyone's life there are things that are most important to them. Mine are, in the following order: my country, my leader Chairman Mao, my family, my Chinese friends. My teachers and student friends. Finally, everyone else.'

During those years in England, from about 1955 to 1963, most of us were proud of the way China had become more important in the world. But we all had different hopes for the future of the nation.

H. H. Tien was a student of mathematics. He was thin and wore thick glasses and, although not very handsome, he was warm, kind and attractive. H. H. was a natural leader and had great hopes for the future of China under Chairman Mao. I argued with him: 'How can you be sure that China will become a great country? If the Chinese people were greedy and dishonest before, have they now changed just because the government is different?'

It was the time of the Cold War.* A few of the most political students were asked to leave Britain because they were 'undesirable'.

---

* Cold War: the years when the countries of the Western world and the Communist countries fought each other for political power.

C. S. married a Singaporean Chinese girl. He took her back to Shanghai and then taught science in Beijing. They later suffered greatly during the Cultural Revolution.* The next time I saw him and his wife, in 1980, C. S. had lost his hair and his love for his country. He asked if I could help him to get a job in America. He did not complain about his decision to return to China, and was still warm, generous, honest and kind.

Others were less fortunate. H. H. was thirty-three and still single when he was told to leave Britain. He went back to China in 1962, against the advice of his parents. Months passed. No one ever heard from him. He had simply disappeared. Years later, we heard that H. H. had been put in prison during the Cultural Revolution. He received horrible treatment at the hands of the people who had put him there. They tried to make him say that he was responsible for all sorts of crimes. H. H. refused, and killed himself in 1967.

His 'disappearance' was difficult and upsetting for us. For me personally, it destroyed any idea of ever returning to work in the country of my birth.

♦

As the years passed, I attended the weddings of many friends, feeling more and more lonely. I had kept my feelings for Karl secret, but while I loved him I was unable to love anyone else.

When I had finished my course in London, I went to Edinburgh, perhaps to try to get away from my impossible relationship with Karl. I spent two years there, continuing my medical studies, and finally realized that I had to leave Britain completely.

It was unspeakably hard to leave Karl. He was my teacher, my

* Cultural Revolution: a movement for political change in China, headed by Mao's Communists, which affected every part of people's lives.

adviser, my first love. But the relationship had failed. In a moment of terrible unhappiness, I destroyed all his letters.

Soon afterwards, in 1963, I left England for Hong Kong.

Chapter 10   Fighting Life's Difficulties Alone

I flew back to Hong Kong with sadness, but also with confidence. I had arranged a good job and housing for myself at the Hong Kong University medical school.

Gregory and James met me at the airport. They were both now working for Father. He paid them each a small amount of money every month and together they rented a one-room apartment above a nightclub in Kowloon.

Hong Kong was not a sleepy city now. The streets were full of people and traffic, even after 9 p.m. There were a great number of new buildings, and colourful electric signs.

'This is not the Hong Kong I left eleven years ago!' I told my brothers.

'I'm glad you've come back,' Gregory said. 'This is the right place and the right time. Everyone is doing well here. Our clever Old Man is making a fortune.'

Father now owned three factories in Hong Kong, and was planning to build another one in Nigeria.

Gregory looked at my old-fashioned dress, which was too large for me, and shook his head. 'If you decide to stay here to work as a doctor, you must dress better. Hong Kong women are very fashionable. Your clothes aren't good enough.'

I was a little upset. 'I've never been beautiful,' I said, 'and I have just got off the plane.'

'She looks all right to me,' said James warmly, putting his arm around my shoulder.

We waited for the lift to take us up to Father and Niang's

45

apartment. I was nervous and fearful, as always when I was going to face my parents. I had spent eleven years in England and was now a doctor, but at that moment I felt just like the schoolgirl who left in 1952.

I was greeted formally. Father looked the same, but Niang had aged. We sat round the large dining table and ate. For some reason, conversation was in English. I told them about the job I had arranged.

'I've been thinking about this,' Father started. 'It's not a good idea. You should work in women's medicine.'

I had forgotten that eleven years ago Father had already decided on the type of work I should do. This was a serious decision about my future, but Father thought the decision was his, not mine. He added that a friend of his, Professor Daphne Chun, worked in women's medicine at the university and would give me a job. The pay was insultingly low. The job was only offered because I was his daughter.

I knew I could not refuse because this would insult Father and his friend. I did try to explain that the job at the medical school was much better and would give me an important position for a young doctor of twenty-six. Father did not listen. I wanted more than anything to please my father. To be accepted by him. To be loved. I could see that he wanted me to take the job with Professor Chun. So once again I followed Father's wishes.

◆

On my fourth day in Hong Kong, Niang told me to pack my bags. We got into the car and the driver took us to Professor Chun's hospital, my new workplace.

The place seemed empty. We talked to the busy hospital operator in the entrance hall. She told us that Dr Chun was not there to show us around, and to return on Monday.

46

But Niang was not satisfied. She ordered the doctor on duty to be called. When a young woman doctor arrived, Niang demanded that she should show me my room. There was no room for me.

'Where do *you* sleep then?' Niang asked loudly, to my embarrassment.

'I sleep in the on-call room,' the young woman answered. When Niang discovered that there were four beds in the room and that two were not being used, she made the woman take us there.

We entered a large room with four beds and little other furniture. There were no curtains at the dirty windows. Niang ordered the driver to place my suitcases by one of the beds, and turned to me. 'Unfortunately, Father and I will be busy all next week. But maybe we could have dinner together next Sunday.'

I was left in that empty room, lonely and sad. I wondered why I had returned home.

♦

My work at the hospital was physically demanding but not very interesting.

Life was difficult. Male doctors earned more than female doctors, although the work was the same. I was not popular. My colleagues did not like me because I was not Cantonese, and because I had studied in London. They thought my English accent was strange. They were annoyed that I was always sleeping in the on-call room. There was nowhere for me to go in the evenings and weekends. Very soon I realized that I had to get away from Hong Kong.

Every Sunday, Gregory, James, Susan and I were expected to have dinner with Father and Niang. Those meals were terribly difficult. Niang seemed to know everything about our lives, especially those matters we did not want her to know. She knew about Gregory's problems with money and parking tickets;

James's drinking; my idea of renting a larger flat for my two brothers and me; Susan's letters to a male American friend. I hated those Sunday nights.

◆

When I had been at the hospital for seven months, a 25-year-old Chinese-American medical student arrived. Martin Ching had come from New York University medical school to spend a month with us.

A couple of times in the evenings after work, Martin and I sat around talking. Martin could speak only a little Cantonese and had experienced the same prejudice as I.

'You're wasting your time here,' he told me. 'You can do the work here with your eyes closed. You had an offer of a better job – why don't you take it?'

I thought of my father and Niang. 'I've got to get out of Hong Kong, Martin.'

'So why don't you come to America? It's easy for a doctor from London University to get a job.'

A new life suddenly opened up before me. America! Anything would be possible there!

'Listen,' Martin said. 'I am going back to New York next week. I'll help you to find a job.'

At that time in America, there were not enough doctors. I wrote to every hospital that Martin suggested. A hospital in Philadelphia wrote back offering me a job immediately, and I accepted. There was just one problem. I did not have the money for an airline ticket.

During Sunday dinner, I bravely told Father and Niang that I had decided to go to America. This was greeted by complete silence. The plan was new to them.

I told them about my problem with the airfare. I wondered whether banks would lend me the money for the ticket. Niang

48

said, 'Well, Adeline, if they won't, that's just too bad.' I understood that they would not help me.

In fact, my new hospital helped me with the airfare, and I left Hong Kong soon afterwards. Gregory and James came to the airport to say goodbye. Half an hour before the plane left, Father rushed in. We waited at the gate and all shook hands. I wanted to tell Father that I had tried hard to please him, but the words did not come. Father said, 'Well, you're truly alone now. Let's see what you can do.'

◆

Martin came to meet me at the airport. I had travelled on the cheapest ticket, and the journey had taken almost forty-eight hours. I was fast asleep in the car. Martin shook me awake when we arrived at the house he shared with a friend. 'Welcome to America, sleepy head!' he said.

Martin carried my two suitcases inside. The house was clean and tidy. A tall young man came out of the lighted kitchen. I was tired, but I noticed that he was very handsome. 'Hi, I'm Byron Bai-lun Soon. I live here in Martin's house.' He spoke with a heavy northern Chinese accent.

Martin and Byron rushed round to make me comfortable. I only wanted to sleep.

Next morning, I slept late. Martin had left the house when I eventually got up. In the living-room, I found Byron, quietly reading an engineering book. He smiled at me. 'I was wondering when you would come down.' In the light of day, he looked even better. 'Shall we have lunch?' he suggested. 'It's all ready.'

We sat at the kitchen table together and ate, and Byron told me about his family. His parents had separated. His mother was still in China, but his father had escaped to Hong Kong with Byron and Arnold, his older brother. The boys had attended Taiwan University, before moving to America for further study.

Byron said he had an evening job at an engineering company and was studying during the day. He had a green card, which allowed him to live and work in America.

'I thought about you all last night,' Byron told me. 'I decided to miss my classes to be with you today. This is going to be my lucky day!'

I was so surprised by the interest that this handsome young man was showing in me. We talked all afternoon. Finally, he stood up to leave me. Gently touching my hair, he said, 'This is the happiest day of my life. I am going to tell you something. Before 1964 is over, you will be my wife.'

I married Byron in New York City, just six weeks after my arrival in America. We had spent less than ten hours alone together.

Chapter 11   Living a Lie

When I thought about my marriage to Byron, I told myself that most arranged marriages in China started the same way. People had to learn to live together. I soon began to learn about Byron.

Two weeks after the wedding, when I was washing clothes, I found a letter in one of Byron's trouser pockets. It was from his bank, telling him that they were closing his bank account. He was in financial difficulties.

Then I telephoned the engineering company where Byron said he worked. They told me that he only worked there occasionally and part time. A call later from someone with a Cantonese accent made it clear that Byron's main employment was as a waiter in a Chinese restaurant.

When I tried to talk to him about these things, he became angry. 'There is nothing to discuss,' he told me. 'I married you, didn't I? What else do you want?'

'I want to understand you, and I hope you'll try to understand me.'

'I don't feel like talking. I want to watch the television.'

'Can we talk afterwards?'

'No! I want you to understand that when I say no I mean no.'

'Am I your wife or your servant? Why can't we talk about things calmly?'

I could feel his growing anger. Without a word, he stood up and walked out.

He did not return until two in the morning. In the long hours waiting for him, I thought about our marriage. I could not divorce him. I could never tell Father and Niang that my marriage had failed. I made up my mind to save my marriage.

The next day, Byron was in a better mood. He happily showed me a letter from his lawyer. It said that his chances of getting a green card were 'very good'. He had forgotten that he had told me he already had a green card. I bit my lip and said nothing.

Byron was looking for a full-time job in engineering. He saw an advertisement in the newspaper. 'Engineers! Come to Southern California, where the sun shines every day!'

So we moved to California. I began working at a California hospital. I was given the use of a small house next to the hospital, and Byron and I moved in there.

Although Byron was very good-looking, I never grew close to him. I believed that if I tried hard enough, love would follow, but unfortunately it never did. We kept a distance between ourselves. This was how Byron wanted the marriage to be. Heart-to-heart conversations made him uncomfortable. We ate our meals in silence; the television was Byron's company.

By October 1965, though, I was expecting a baby. Byron seemed pleased that he was going to be a father. I decided to become an anaesthetist, as I could then work in a hospital all the time. It was a job which carried a lot of responsibility, and it was very well paid.

The baby was expected at the beginning of June. Byron and I prepared to move out of our house at the hospital and to buy a new house in Fountain Valley, sixteen kilometres away.

We were both very happy to be buying our own home. We wanted to put down roots in America. That evening when the agreement was signed, I cooked a celebratory meal. Over the meal we began to have a discussion about our green cards. Byron had now received his, and could live in America for ever. 'You should go to a lawyer,' he told me, 'and get yours as soon as possible. Why didn't you do it when we first met?'

'When we first met, you had no green card yourself,' I said without thinking.

His face darkened. 'Are you calling me a liar?'

'You know very well that you didn't have a green card when we met at Martin Ching's house,' I said.

Suddenly, he became very angry. He stood up and began to shout, 'If you still want Martin, why don't you go and find him in New York?'

At that moment, the telephone rang. The hospital operator was unable to find the doctor on call. Could I come in immediately to help two patients who had been in a car accident? I rushed out of the house.

Four hours later, I returned. I was very tired. My feet were aching and I kicked off my shoes before turning on the light. An unbelievable scene met my eyes. In his anger Byron had pulled out all the drawers and emptied everything on the floor in the middle of the living room. Clothes, plates, books and food had been thrown everywhere. In the kitchen, dirty dishes were spread across the table and in the sink. Byron was not there.

I cleared the kitchen and then started on the mess in the living room. 'At least he didn't burn the house down,' I told myself.

Towards six in the morning, a key turned in the lock and Byron entered. He walked into the bedroom, packed a small bag and hurried out again without a word.

He was gone for five days. I believed my marriage had ended. The baby was expected in two weeks. I continued working, which gave me a little happiness.

Then suddenly, he came back. I came home one evening and found him watching television. I cooked dinner and we ate in silence.

My pains began at seven in the morning of 8 June 1966. Byron looked after me. He walked me to the hospital and sat by my bedside. Our son, Roger, was born that evening, beautiful and healthy.

I gave all my love to our wonderful baby. I rushed home from work to bath and feed him. I felt very lucky to be able to give him the love I had missed when I was a child. Our marriage was a pretence, but we appeared to be a nice, happy Chinese-American family.

On New Year's Day, 1967, we went to a new shopping centre to buy a suit for Byron. In the men's shop, he was trying on a jacket when the salesman tried to tell him that it was too large. Byron turned to me, 'What do you think of the jacket?'

Without thinking, I said, 'I think he's right. It's too big. Why don't you try a smaller size?'

Byron looked angrily at me. Then, without a word, he took off the jacket, turned and walked out of the shop.

I waited for Byron for two hours in the car. I phoned Mrs Hsu, who looked after Roger, but he had not returned. I drove home.

We had planned a dinner party for that evening. I did not know what to do. Finally, I phoned all the guests and told them not to come because Byron was ill.

Much later, I heard Byron's key in the front door. He came into the room.

'Where are my guests?' he asked.

'I didn't know whether you were coming home,' I replied, 'So I told them not to come.'

'Who gave you permission to do that? They are *my* guests!' he shouted.

I did not answer, for fear of making him more angry. I walked into the bathroom.

The next minute I heard a bedroom door being thrown open, the breaking of furniture and a cry of terror from my baby. I ran into the baby's room and saw Byron standing over the screaming six-month-old child in his broken bed. I felt ready to murder him. I picked up my crying son, marched into our bedroom and locked the door.

Next I heard a loud crash from the kitchen. Then the front door shut and Byron was gone. I looked carefully at my baby and found that he was not badly hurt. In the kitchen, Mrs Hsu was looking fearfully at the broken dishes and food everywhere. Byron had lifted the table and thrown everything on the floor.

This time he stayed away for a week. When he returned, I made it clear that I wanted him to sleep in the guest room upstairs. From that time, Byron became more violent to me and to our baby. At work I lied to my colleagues about my black eyes. I did not want people to know that our marriage was at an end.

◆

In October of 1970, Father and Niang were on a world trip and decided to visit us.

During their visit, I tried to pretend that all was well in my life: job, home life, health, money, lovely son, handsome husband. But they were watching us carefully. Father had noticed that Byron was able to use my money as he liked. He gave me some advice. 'You must pay attention to money matters. You have a well-paid job. If you're careful, you have the opportunity to build up a large fortune. You must arrange things so that you have control over your own money. People change and their feelings change too.' I was shocked by this unexpected advice. They had understood what my marriage was really like.

Niang agreed with Father. 'Your husband,' she suddenly asked, 'is he all right in the head? Is he perhaps a little crazy?' I was surprised. I had often wondered about this.

'You told me you were thinking of buying some property,' Father said. 'You must see a good lawyer and make sure it is in your name alone. Do you hear?'

My eyes filled with tears. Father was trying to protect me.

Niang added, 'Remember, your parents will always be your parents. Listen to your father and do what he says.' Those were the kindest words she ever said to me.

I understood that they were telling me that I should get a divorce. I decided to see a lawyer immediately.

Byron agreed to the divorce if I gave him our house and if I made no demand for money to support our child. I agreed immediately and moved into another house. After the divorce, Byron did not write to or see his son again.

Chapter 12   Discovering Heaven in Marriage

In 1965, Father opened a factory in Nigeria. Machinery and hundreds of people were moved out there. Housing was built for the Chinese workers next to the new factory.

That same year Gregory married Matilda, a Chinese girl, and Father made him manager of the Nigerian factory. Soon after their wedding, they moved to Nigeria. Away from family and friends, Gregory found life in Africa difficult and lonely. When Matilda was expecting a baby, Gregory wrote to Father. He suggested that they should both return to Canada to try to become Canadian citizens. They had both been students there. Their baby could be born there. James could run the factory for a short time.

Father wrote to say that he had already decided to give James Gregory's job. His letter continued, 'You have been spending too much of the company's money.' Father had been told that Gregory and Matilda had spent extra money on food and drink, and had once slept for a short time after lunch to escape the heat of a West African afternoon. Father ended his letter by demanding that they explain their wasteful behaviour. Not a word of thanks for all of Gregory's hard work.

After Gregory and Matilda left for Canada, James helped Father to run his businesses. For ten years, he worked at the factory in Nigeria. He was married, but his wife Louise stayed in Hong Kong with their children. He was allowed to come home to his family only twice a year, from Christmas to Chinese New Year and in the summer. This was the time when Father and Niang went to Monte Carlo to stay in the flat they had bought overlooking the Mediterranean. James took care of the business in Father's absence.

◆

In 1969, Edgar moved to Canada, but there were few well-paid jobs there. He decided to join me in California and asked me to find him work at my hospital. Father advised me that it would not be a good idea to have Edgar so close to me, and I did not help him. Edgar was offended and never forgave me.

He moved from city to city in California and then to Hong Kong. His marriage was unhappy. He finally returned to California, divorced his wife and married his office nurse. They had three daughters and appeared happy.

◆

When Susan finished college in America, she returned to Hong Kong. She worked as a schoolteacher and lived at home with our parents. They wanted her to marry. Susan was very beautiful and had many admirers. Niang wanted to hear everything about them. She questioned every move, every letter, every phone call that Susan made. Susan hated this. Finally, they had a terrible argument. Father was so upset by this that eventually Susan apologized to Niang.

Soon after that, Susan met Tony Liang, the son of a successful businessman, and they decided to get married. The wedding was small and private. Father and Niang did not attend. Susan received no money or presents from them.

Tony did well in business and the young Liangs became well known in Hong Kong society. Niang was jealous and criticized Susan's clothes, jewellery and behaviour.

Eventually Susan and Niang had another argument, even more terrible than the first. Niang told her that she wished Susan had died instead of Franklin. Susan replied that Niang loved no one except herself. Niang hit Susan across the face, and told her to get out.

Susan met Father for lunch the next week. He read to Susan from a piece of paper with Niang's writing on. It was a list of rules and conditions that Susan must agree to follow if she wished to stay a member of the Yen family. Susan shook her head.

Father put some money on the table. 'I shall give your mother your message.' The look on his face upset Susan deeply.

Four of us were living abroad at this time, and we received the news in a letter from Father and Niang. 'We wish to inform you that Susan is no longer part of the Yen family. You are not to speak or write to her again.'

That is how my half-sister Susan was disowned in 1973.

♦

In Shanghai, Aunt Baba had continued working at the Women's Bank. She stayed in the house with Miss Chien, Franklin's teacher. After a time Aunt Baba discovered that Miss Chien had stolen cotton, wool and food. She reported this in a letter to Father, and asked him to send Miss Chien away. Father replied with an order that Miss Chien must stay. My aunt need not worry about 'missing' things. Clearly Father had secret reasons for this.

Aunt Baba and Miss Chien stopped speaking to each other. Aunt Baba lived in the top part of the house, while Miss Chien entertained her family and friends downstairs. She talked to the neighbours and whispered that she was sending secret 'weekly progress reports' on Aunt Baba's life to Father, her employer, in Hong Kong.

The government was beginning to take control of every part of citizens' lives, through groups at work and at home who spied on people all the time. They were looking for any behaviour that was against the ideas of the Communist Party. People outside the Party were attacked for such crimes as waste, or not paying taxes. Aunt Baba was questioned about her family business. She and her friends were not allowed to play their favourite game, *mah-jong*.

My grandaunt, too, was having a difficult time. Meetings were started against her to 'help her to understand her past mistakes and to correct them'. Many of her old employees spoke against her, wanting to save themselves. She was found guilty of activities against the Party and was forced to give up her duties at the Women's Bank. She was allowed to stay in her apartment, but everything else was taken from her. She was not allowed to use the lift in the building, although she had pains in the chest from climbing up and down the stairs.

Aunt Baba was often made to work at banks far from home. She had to travel long distances on crowded buses. She too became ill, with pains in the stomach. A doctor gave her some medicine and advised her to stop working.

Aunt Baba wrote to Father and asked him to send money each month for her support. Father agreed. The years between 1959 and 1966 were peaceful for Aunt Baba. She did not have to rush to work in the mornings. There were fewer political meetings. There was more food. She could meet her friends during the day.

Then, in the summer of 1966, groups of local Red Guards walked the streets of Shanghai looking for trouble. They attacked people and stole from shops and homes. Aunt Baba did not dare go out.

One day, twenty-five Red Guards knocked loudly on the door of Aunt Baba's house. They were teenage boys and girls and a few men in their twenties. They made everyone get down on the floor. They hit Miss Chien so hard that two of her teeth were knocked out. Then they attacked my aunt. They broke her false teeth, pulled her hair and whipped her with their belts.

They built a fire in the garden and burnt all the books, photographs and paintings. They were very angry when they found no money or jewellery, and before they left they broke furniture, pulled down curtains and cut up clothes. Miss Chien was ordered to move out within twenty-four hours, and to go back to Hangzhou where she came from.

Afterwards, for the first time in fifteen years, Miss Chien spoke nicely to my aunt. She said that she was deeply sorry about what had happened. My aunt gave her an old suitcase and she left.

A week later, Aunt Baba was made to move into a single room at a neighbour's house. Other families moved into her house. She could not take money from her bank, and mail from Father was not delivered. The government gave her a very small amount of money to live on.

In 1972, life improved greatly for ordinary Chinese. There was more food and fewer public meetings. Aunt Baba was again allowed to receive money from Father. He also now sent money to Grand Aunt, who had often been cold and hungry, and he continued to send it until her death three years later.

In 1976, Mao Zedong died. New leaders took power and China's doors started to open to the outside world.

♦

After my divorce, my work continued to go well. I was very well paid as an anaesthetist. Success at work, though, did not make me forget my failed marriage. My life felt empty.

A good friend understood this and decided to do something about it. She introduced me to Professor Robert Mah, a Chinese-American university teacher.

Bob was rather handsome and quite tall, with thick black hair. He was born in California, the youngest of eight children, and had never been to China. I compared the love in his family with the jealousy and arguments in my own family.

When Bob first invited me to dinner, I found that he had spent two days preparing the meal. As we shared this meal, prepared with so much love, I began to hope that we were meant for each other.

That evening I told him about my life as a child. I could not stop talking. He sat holding my hand as I poured out all my pain. I told him how much I desired to make my parents proud of me.

I was only able to see Bob on my rare free evenings, and often I was called away from him by patients. But when I returned home, I always found dinner cooked and Bob waiting for me. In my whole life, I had never found anyone so caring. He was good to me and to my son. He showed his love not by words, but by everything he did.

We were soon married and moved into a beautiful home in Huntington Beach. Our daughter, Ann, was born two years later. I felt that I had come home at last.

Chapter 13 Living on Cheap Tea and Plain Rice

In early 1977, I received a letter from Niang. Father's health was not good. He was becoming more and more confused and had difficulty writing. He had been advised to go to Stanford University for a medical examination. I invited them to stay with us in our new home.

We drove to the airport to meet them. I cried when I saw Father looking so thin and weak, his hair completely white. There was an empty, frightened look in his eyes. Niang looked much older than her fifty-six years.

When we reached our house, our two children, Roger and Ann, ran excitedly towards us to greet their grandparents.

Father entered the house, stopped and gave a small sound of pleasure at the beautiful view through our hallway out over the sea. Niang was cross. 'Go in and sit down, Joseph,' she said. 'What are you looking at? It's *only* Adeline's house.'

Bob and I flew to San Francisco with them. Father stayed at the medical centre for a few days and many tests were performed. The doctor asked Father some questions. He was unable to solve mathematical problems that used to be easy for him. He asked the doctor sadly, 'Why is everything so difficult for me? Why, doctor?'

'I am afraid it is just part of getting old,' the doctor replied. Then he asked Father another question. 'Mr Yen, how many children do you have?'

Father paused. Twice he tried to answer but could not. Tears ran down my face. It hurt so much to see him like this.

We were all back at Huntington Beach when the results of the tests arrived. The news was bad. Father was suffering from Alzheimer's disease, which was affecting his brain. The condition would slowly get worse, leaving Father like a human vegetable. There was no treatment.

My personal relationship with Niang improved after this visit. Bob and I had paid all Father's medical bills, around $50,000, and perhaps she was grateful for this. As a doctor, I knew about the problems that an illness like Father's brought with it, and I understood how difficult this was for her.

◆

China was now open to tourism, and in 1979 Bob and I were asked by American friends to join them on an organized tour of the country.

The thought of seeing Aunt Baba again filled me with emotion. For a long time my letters had not reached her. The Chinese government had made this impossible since the beginning of the Cultural Revolution.

We flew into Shanghai, and as the bus took us towards our hotel, I was excited at seeing the city once again. Bob and I dropped our luggage at the hotel and immediately took a taxi to visit my aunt. She had lived in a room at a neighbour's house in the same road since 1966. It had once been a grand building but was now in a very bad state. Its front door stood open for the world to enter.

The smell hit us as we stepped into the hallway. It was the smell of bad food, unwashed bodies and clothes. Rubbish covered the stairs and hallway.

I slowly climbed the stairs and called out 'Aunt Baba! Aunt Baba!' Then she stood there, a slight figure in the doorway. How small she was! I pressed her tightly to me and felt her bony body.

She led us into her room and made us sit down on the bed. She looked at us, her eyes shining proudly.

The room was cold and dark. The only furniture was a bed, a wooden table and one chair. She felt very lucky to have her own room, as whole families often had to share one room.

I held her small hand while we told the stories of our lives, trying to bridge the thirty years that separated us. My aunt's voice dropped to a whisper. 'I can't believe that we are sitting in this room together discussing all these things. Conversations like this were dangerous even three years ago.'

We talked until late at night. She told the story of our family and asked me to write down these memories. She did not want everything to be forgotten with time. 'Our whole family suffered when your stepmother entered our home. She was young and beautiful and this gave her power over your father.'

I asked her if she was sorry that she had stayed behind in Shanghai. Her answer was no. 'It has been bad here. We have been poor, and afraid, and life has been hard. Quite honestly, though, all these problems together were better than living under the same roof as your Niang. I am happy with cheap tea and plain rice.'

Our eyes met. I saw fearlessness in hers.

♦

Father was now in hospital in Hong Kong. Niang employed three nurses for him during the day and two at night.

Susan was upset when she heard that he was in hospital. She went to see him in his private room, but it was too late. Father did not recognize her. His nurses reported Susan's visit to Niang, who was very angry. She warned her not to try to visit Father again.

My brothers were unhappy that Niang had put all of Father's bank accounts into her own name. They talked about taking legal action against Niang, but I was against this. 'Forget it. At this moment Niang needs our support.'

In May 1988, James phoned to say that Father had become worse and was not expected to live for more than twenty-four hours. I called Lydia in Tianjin, thinking that no one else would inform her. 'Nobody ever remembers me,' she complained. 'I'll probably get nothing from Father's will.' 'Don't worry Lydia,' I said, 'I'll share what I get with you.' Father died a few hours later.

We all flew to Hong Kong for the funeral. The only other people there were the nurses and Mr Lu, Father's chief financial officer. No friends came. Gregory and I had both informed Susan of Father's death, but Niang had not invited her and had left her name out of the newspaper notices.

When the funeral ended, we met at Johnson, Stokes & Masters for the reading of Father's will. The last time we were all together was forty years ago in Shanghai.

When the young lawyer read out the first page of Father's will and then informed us that Father had left no money, we all looked at each other in shocked surprise. We turned to Niang. She calmly looked back at us one by one.

Although we knew that Father's bank accounts were now in her name, we found it unbelievable that she had taken everything else as well: gold, houses, office buildings, land . . . Father had truly died penniless.

◆

After dinner that night, Lydia returned with me to my hotel. She wished to spend the night with me. We changed into our nightdresses and got into our separate beds. By the light of the night-lamp on the small table between us, I could see there was a strange look on Lydia's face. Then she began to speak, and the hurt and anger of her life came pouring out in words.

First she blamed me for not helping her daughter, Tai-ling. I had given her son money to study in America, and at the time she had been full of love and thanks. She now said it was wrong that I had not given her daughter the same amount of money.

A flood of insults hit me. A war of words began.

'What's happening between us? What do you have against me?' I asked.

'These days you behave like a queen and I feel like your servant.' So she continued, without stopping. She was a strange and unhappy woman.

At about three in the morning, I had heard enough.

'If this is how you truly feel about me, then let's put a stop to it. Let's make a break with each other.'

Lydia turned her back and started to cry. After a time her crying stopped and she fell asleep. I suddenly realized that her only purpose for coming tonight was to end her relationship with me.

Two days later, I flew home to Los Angeles. I was very tired and fearful about the future.

Chapter 14   Falling Leaves Return to Their Roots

One year later, when I called Niang in July, 1989, she was not at home. I was told that she was in hospital. After Father's death, Niang had become ill.

I telephoned her room at the hospital. 'Oh, hello, Adeline!' She sounded cool and polite. 'How did you get my number?'

Thousands of kilometres away, I sat up straight in my chair. 'They gave it to me when I called your home. How are you? Would you like me to fly over and look after you?'

She told me that she was having tests for cancer. Then she added, 'I'm feeling fine and can go home in a few days. There is no need for you to come. I don't need your help.'

I rang James to tell him about Niang's illness. 'I offered to fly back to look after her, but she didn't want me. I can't understand why Niang is acting so coldly towards me. Have I offended her in some way?'

James tried not to answer the question. 'It's probably just her illness,' he told me.

The results of Niang's tests showed that she did have cancer and needed an operation. Again, I offered to be with her. James told me quietly but firmly, 'She doesn't want you to come.'

A few days after her operation, though, she phoned to invite my whole family to Hong Kong for a Christmas visit. She sounded friendly.

Bob and I took our two children and spent a happy Christmas with Niang. We celebrated together and exchanged presents.

During the next eight months, Niang's illness worsened. She called me quite frequently, and talked about coming to America.

One day when I phoned, I was told that Niang was back in hospital. She had suddenly felt weak and was unable to walk. I telephoned James, who was in Boston. He flew back to Hong Kong and phoned me from the hospital. He told me that Niang had not recognized him. She was dying.

Niang, on her deathbed, was ready to play her last card. Of her own two children, one was dead and the other disowned. But she was left with five stepchildren to play her final game with. We knew that she held a fortune in her hands. At one time the Yen family was one of the richest in Hong Kong. James told us that she would leave around thirty million US dollars. But who to?

For me, the important thing was not the money itself. Bob and I both had good jobs. It came from a deeper need: to be accepted and loved, to be included in my family. I did not like the idea of any of us being left out. Although I knew that Niang was not good or kind, I wanted her acceptance, as I had wanted Father's.

Another week passed. On Sunday, 9 September, James left a message on our answering machine. 'The Old Lady died an hour and a half ago.'

♦

Few people came to say a last goodbye to Niang as her body lay waiting for the funeral. Mr Lu, Father's loyal employee, told us, 'I don't think anyone else is coming. She had no true friends. She didn't like many people. Look how she cut Susan out of her life and her will, and Susan was her only daughter.'

I looked hard at Mr Lu, trying to read the meaning in his words. 'What are you trying to tell us, Mr Lu?' I asked.

'Your Niang did not want you to know this, but you may get nothing when the will is read tomorrow,' he said.

'I don't believe you!' I cried. 'Just three weeks ago, she asked me to take her to my home in America! Surely she had some feeling for me if she wanted to die in my home.'

Mr Lu shook his head. 'Niang knew that if she died in America, the American government would be able to tax all the money she left. The rest of the family would blame you for taking her to your home to die.'

I began to shake. I was six years old again and it was Chinese New Year. Dressed in bright new clothes, we children ate our special lunch. The sounds of celebration came from outside. One by one, my brothers and sisters were handed the traditional red paper package with gold letters saying 'Happy New Year' and containing money. Everyone except me. That was my punishment for criticizing Niang's beating of baby Susan.

◆

I did not go to the reading of the will. James arrived with my copy later.

'What does it say?' I asked him.

'Gregory and Edgar each get a good share. I get half. Lydia gets a little. Susan gets nothing. You get nothing.'

I looked through the pages and found my name. '*Adeline Yen Mah*,' I read. '*My daughter, Adeline Yen Mah, will receive no part of my money.* Why James, why? Why did she hate me so much?'

'That's how the Old Lady wanted it in the end,' James said. 'Who knows why?'

◆

I decided to find out what was in Father's will, the will that Niang had not allowed us to see. Bob and I went to Niang's flat the following day.

I went into Niang's bedroom. I felt ill when I saw and smelt her personal belongings. I looked in her clothes cupboard, but found nothing. Then I looked in her old Chinese desk. I pulled open the top drawer.

There were piles and piles of letters inside. Perhaps two hundred letters. I looked at the familiar small handwriting on the envelopes. All were addressed to Mrs Joseph Yen and all were written by Lydia.

Why was Lydia writing to Niang almost every two days? I pulled out the top letter from its envelope. As I started to read, a pain tightened my chest. Letter after letter was filled with lies and poison against me. Lydia called me 'cruel, selfish and mean'. She said I had disobeyed Niang's wishes and stayed in contact with Susan. She said that I told James to leave the country and leave Niang. It continued like this, letter after letter.

From next door I heard a shout from Bob. He had found Father's will. We sat on Niang's bed together and read it again and again.

My father's will was very different from the one written by Niang less than three weeks after his death. He left one share to me, one share to Gregory, one share to Edgar, two shares to James and two shares to his grandchildren with the last name of Yen. Susan got nothing. Father also wrote in his will the following sentence: '*None of my money will go to my daughter, Lydia Yen Sung.*'

I held Bob tightly. 'In the end, Niang's will doesn't matter.

This, my father's will, is what is important to me. He did not forget me. Perhaps he loved me after all.'

◆

One day in March 1994, I received a letter from my aunt asking me to go to her in Shanghai. Inside me, a quiet, small voice whispered that this visit would be the last.

Once again, I entered the familiar road. Aunt Baba had returned to live in the old family house. Now it was bright and newly painted.

My aunt was lying in her bed. To my surprise, she was cheerful, although very ill. She was surrounded by neighbours and friends who were at her bedside day and night. Her life was like a continuous goodbye party.

I had returned to the warmth of Aunt Baba's world, safe in the knowledge that I was always important to her. Holding her hand, I forgot the worries and fears that had been in my head since I learned of her illness. She was peaceful and happy. She refused any idea of going into hospital.

'I have had a good eighty-nine years. It is time to accept the end.'

Her only worry was for the loved ones she must leave behind. She wanted to give me strength after all my hurt. I lay on the bed next to her thin, weak body. . . the way I used to as a child when I could not sleep. She touched my hair gently and told me stories.

Day after day, as I sat beside her, I believed that my presence would help her along her final journey. I thought about the eighty-nine years of her life, and realized how wise my mother had been to give me to the care of my wonderful aunt. In her quiet way, she had guided me to independence. Aunt Baba was not angry about the difficulties she had suffered. Love, kindness and humour never left her.

Life had come full circle. Falling leaves return to their roots.

ACTIVITIES

Chapters 1–2

Before you read

1 Read the Introduction to the book. Use the Internet, books and your own knowledge to answer these questions.

    a Adeline, the writer of this book, and the main character, was born in China in 1937. What was China like then? What were its most important cities? How did rich and poor people live?

    b What happened to China during the Second World War (1939–1945)?

    c China has gone through many changes during the last twenty years. What is the country like now? Would you like to visit the country? Why (not)?

    d Adeline's family moved to Hong Kong. Find out about the island's history. What made the area so rich? Why did the British government return the island to the Chinese in 1997?

2 Look at the Word List at the back of the book. Use some of the words in these sentences.

    a After the old woman's .... the .... read her .... to the family.

    b Because the child was an ...., she was sent to .... in a school run by ....

    c After my father married my ...., she demanded total .... If I made her angry, she .... me until my skin bled.

    d All plants, including .... and ...., have ....

    e The .... was .... at the hospital three nights a week.

    f After I .... my wife, my father .... me and refused to speak to me.

3 The Chinese had a custom of binding women's feet. Why do you think they did this? When do you think this custom stopped?

4 In this story, parts of China are affected by dangerous floods. Are there ever floods in your country? What causes them? What are the effects?

While you read

5 What are the relationships between these people?

a Susan is Adeline's   ....

b Jeanne Prosperi is Joseph's   ....

c Lydia is Adoline's   ....

d Jeanne is Adeline's   ....

e Ye Ye is Adeline's   ....

f Baba is Adeline's   ....

g Miss Ren is Joseph's   ....

h Mrs Prosperi is Jeanne's   ....

i Pierre is Jeanne's   ....

j Franklin is Adeline's   ....

After you read

6 Match each of these events with the correct date.

1903 1911 1924 1930 1937 1939 1941 1988

a Adeline's father marries her mother.   .....

b Adeline's half-sister is born.   .....

c Adeline's grandparents marry.   .....

d Adeline's father leaves home and joins the family business.   .....

e Adeline is born.   .....

f Adeline's father dies.   .....

g Dr Sun Yat Sen becomes President of China.   .....

h A flood hits Tianjin and many people are killed.   .....

7 Work with another student. Discuss:

a Father's reasons for marrying Jeanne. Why does he like her? What is special about her?

b Jeanne's history. Has she had an easy childhood? Why (not)? What do you know about her family?

c Father and Jeanne's wedding. Why are the children not invited? How do you think this makes them feel?

Chapters 3–5

Before you read

8 Discuss these questions.

    a *Niang* is a Chinese word for mother. Do you think that Niang will behave as a real mother would towards her stepchildren? Why (not)?

    b Adeline was born in 1937. The next three chapters cover the time from 1941 to 1948. What do you think will happen to her during these years? Do you think she will have a happy childhood?

While you read

9 Who:

    a is 'a rather frightening figure' to Adeline? ....

    b is 'full of life'? ....

    c is a bully? ....

    d is Adeline's favourite brother? ....

    e 'disappears' to Shanghai? ....

    f dies in 1943? ....

    g beats baby Susan? ....

    h gives money to the children? ....

    i goes back to work in a bank? ....

    j is sent to school in Tianjin? ....

After you read

10 Discuss why these are important to the story:

    a tram fares

    b the children's haircuts

    c Adeline's duckling

    d Lydia's damaged arm

11 Work with another student. Have this conversation.

    Student A: You are Adeline. It is the day after your school friends came to your house. Tell your special friend Wu Chun-mei about your life with Niang and Father.

Student B: You are Wu Chun-mei. Ask Adeline about her family and her problems. Can you suggest ways to help her?

Chapters 6–8

Before you read

12 Father wants to send Adeline away to school. He says that she is 'difficult' and 'must be taught a lesson'. Why is he so hard towards her? Why can't he love her in the same way he loves his sons? Give reasons for your answer.

13 Look at the titles of Chapter 7 and Chapter 8. Adeline dreams of 'magic lands' and 'a brighter future'. What do you think she wants for her future? Discuss your thoughts with other students.

While you read

14 Circle the correct answers.

   a St Joseph's School is in *Tianjin / Shanghai*.

   b Niang's *cousin / sister* visits Adeline at school.

   c Adeline goes to her family in *Hong Kong / Tianjin*. ✤

   d Aunt Reine hides Niang's diamonds in her *coat / bag*.

   e Ye Ye is *happy / unhappy* in Hong Kong.

   f Niang wants Adeline to be a *secretary / teacher*.

   g Adeline wins a prize for a play in *English / Chinese*.

   h Adeline wants to study *medicine / literature*.

   i In 1949 Lydia and her family escape to *Tianjin / Taiwan*.

   j When Adeline leaves for England, she is full of *hope / unhappiness*.

After you read

15 Complete these sentences.

   a Many girls leave St Joseph's School because …

   b Aunt Reine visits Adeline at school and …

   c After Gregory and Edgar finish school, they …

   d James and Uncle Frederick do not have papers for Hong Kong so …

    e Father makes a name for himself in Hong Kong by ...

    f Mary Suen is kind to Adeline because ...

    g Ye Ye is lonely in Hong Kong because ...

    h Adeline's luck changes after ...

    i After Samuel and Lydia return to Tianjin, Samuel ...

    j In 1952 Adeline is full of hope because ...

16 Imagine that you are Aunt Reine and you visit Adeline at school. Think of ten questions that you would ask her about her life at school and at home. Compare your list with another student.

Chapters 9–11

Before you read

17 Discuss these questions.

    a Adeline and her brothers Gregory and Edgar go to London to study in the 1950s. What do you think life was like in England at this time for students from other countries? Do you think the situation is different now? If so, why?

    b In the 1960s Chairman Mao Zedong led a movement called the Cultural Revolution. Find out about this time in Chinese history. What was life like for ordinary Chinese people in the cities and in the countryside? What happened to people who did not support Chairman Mao?

While you read

18 Are these sentences true (T) or false (F)?

    a Franklin probably dies because he eats unwashed strawberries. .....

    b Gregory studies medicine in London. .....

    c Female medical students face prejudice at university. .....

    d Adeline's relationship with Karl Decker has to be kept secret. .....

    e Adeline leaves England because Karl wants to marry her. .....

f Father is unhappy about the job that Adeline has
arranged for herself in Hong Kong. .....

g Adeline enjoys her work in women's medicine. .....

h Adeline gets a job at a hospital in New York. .....

i Adeline's husband becomes violent and difficult to
live with. .....

j Father and Niang want Adeline to divorce her husband. .....

After you read

19 Put these events in the correct order.

a Adeline falls in love with Karl Decker.

b Adeline starts studying at University College, London.

c Adeline has a baby son.

d Adeline completes her medical studies in Scotland.

e Adeline gets a job in Philadelphia in the United States.

f Adeline goes to England.

g Adeline marries Byron Bai-lun Soon.

h Adeline goes to work in a hospital in California.

i Adeline returns to Hong Kong.

j Adeline divorces her husband.

20 Adeline experiences racial and sexual prejudice in England in the
1950s. Why were people insulting and rude to foreigners? Why did
they insult the female students? Have attitudes changed, do you
think? Why (not)? Discuss your answers with other students.

21 Work with another student. It is the day Adeline and Byron sign
the agreement to buy their new house. Have this conversation.

Student A: You are Adeline. You have discovered that your
husband lied to you about his green card. You and
Byron have argued. Byron has damaged the house,
then packed a bag and left home. Ring your friend
Martin Ching and tell him about your problems.

Student B: You are Martin. Talk to Adeline about her arguments
with Byron. Find out why they disagree. Ask questions
about their relationship. What do you think Adeline
should do next?

Chapters 12–14

Before you read

22 What do you think will happen next to Adeline? Will she find happiness in her life? Do you think she will leave America and return to Hong Kong or China?

23 In the next three chapters, who do you think:

   a will be disowned by the Yen family?

   Susan   Adeline   James

   b will marry for a second time?

   Niang   Susan   Adeline

   c will suffer from a brain disease?

   Father   Niang   Aunt Baba

   d will hide Father's will from his children?

   Aunt Baba   Lydia   Niang

While you read

24 Choose the correct ending for each sentence. Write the correct numbers.

   a Father advises Adeline not to help …   .....

   b Niang and Susan have …   .....

   c The Chinese government takes …   .....

   d Aunt Baba is attacked …   .....

   e Adeline is successful …   .....

   f Bob is very kind …   .....

   g Susan is not invited …   .....

   h Lydia wrote …   .....

   1) terrible arguments.

   2) unkind letters about Adeline to Niang.

   3) by the Red Guards.

   4) Edgar find a job.

   5) to Adeline and her son.

   6) control of people's lives.

   7) to her father's funeral.

   8) in her work as an anaesthetist.

After you read

25 Work with another student. Have this conversation.

    Student A: You are Adeline. Tell Bob about the differences between Father's will and the will that Niang wrote after Father's death. Explain why the first will is so important to you.

    Student B: You are Bob. Talk to Adeline about her relationship with her brothers and sisters. Discuss the importance of the will with her.

26 In the last line of the book, Adeline Yen Mah says: 'Falling leaves return to their roots.' Discuss the meaning of this sentence with another student. In what ways does Adeline return to her roots? Why has the writer chosen 'falling leaves' as the title for this book?

Writing

27 Adeline has won first prize in a play-writing competition. You are a journalist. Write a report for your newspaper about her win. Include information about her family and background.

28 You are Ye Ye. Your life is coming to an end. Write about your best and worst years and your relationship with your family.

29 You are Adeline. You are seventeen and you are studying medicine in London. Write your diary. Write about your experiences with the other students and your secret friendship with Dr Karl Decker.

30 You are Adeline and you are preparing to move from London to Edinburgh. Write a letter to Karl Decker. Explain your feelings for him and your reasons for leaving England.

31 Adeline's father has just died. Write about his life for a newspaper. Explain how he became rich and why he moved from China to Hong Kong.

32 Write life stories for Adeline's brothers and sisters (including Franklin and Susan). Describe their characters and what happens to them.

33 You are Aunt Baba. You are very ill and know that soon you will die. Write a letter to Adeline explaining how much you loved her. Describe your own life and your experiences in China during the rule of Chairman Mao Zedong.

34 Write Niang's will in a way that you think is fair. Give reasons for your decisions.

35 Write one of Lydia's letters to Niang, talking about Adeline. Remember that you hate Adeline and want Niang to dislike her too.

36 Write a letter to the writer telling her your thoughts about this book. Which parts affected you most strongly?

WORD LIST

anaesthetist (n) a doctor who stops people feeling pain during operations

bank account (n) an arrangement that allows you to keep your money in a bank and take it out when you need it

bind (v) to tie something tightly

board (v) to get on a ship; to live at a school

bully (n/v) someone who uses their strength or power to frighten or hit other people

cancer (n) a serious disease that can spread through your body

chairman (n) the leader of a meeting, group or company; the title given to Mao Zedong as the Chinese leader

concubine (n) a woman who, in the past, had a relationship like a marriage with a man

disown (v) to say that a person doesn't belong to your family now

divorce (n/v) the legal end of a marriage

duckling (n) a baby duck; a duck is a water bird which is killed for its meat

flood (n) a very large amount of water that covers an area which is usually dry

funeral (n) a formal event for a person who has just died

grandaunt (n) the sister of your grandfather or grandmother

lawyer (n) someone who advises people about the law and helps them in court

magnolia (n) a tree with large pink or white flowers

medal (n) a round, flat piece of metal given as a prize to the winner of a competition

nun (n) a woman who lives in a group of religious women, separately from other people

obedience (n) the act of obeying a person or rule

on call (phrase) ready to go to work if you are needed

orphan (n) a child with no living parents

pocket money (n) regular sums of money that children are given by their parents or carers

prejudice (n) unfair dislike of someone who is different in some way

professor (n) a teacher at a college or university

roots (n pl) the parts of a plant that grow under the ground; the beginnings of something. When you put down roots in a place, you make it your home.

stepmother (n) a woman who is married to your father but is not your mother

strawberry (n) a small, red, juicy fruit that grows on plants near the ground

tram (n) a passenger vehicle powered by electricity

whip (n/v) a long, thin piece of leather, for example, with a handle, used for hitting people or animals

will (n) a legal document in which you say what should happen to your property after you die